LIVES OF GREAT RELIGIOUS BOOKS

The *Koran* in English

LIVES OF GREAT RELIGIOUS BOOKS

FORTHCOMING

The *Koran* in English

A BIOGRAPHY

Bruce B. Lawrence

PRINCETON UNIVERSITY PRESS

Princeton and Oxford

Copyright © 2017 by Princeton University Press

Published by Princeton University Press, 41 William Street, Princeton,
New Jersey 08540
In the United Kingdom: Princeton University Press, 6 Oxford Street,
Woodstock, Oxfordshire OX20 1TR

press.princeton.edu

Jacket art: Initial panel from *American Qur'an* (Sandow Birk). Courtesy
of the Catherine Clark Gallery of San Francisco and Sandow Birk

Library of Congress Cataloging-in-Publication Data

Names: Lawrence, Bruce B., author.
Title: The Koran in English : a biography / Bruce B. Lawrence.
Description: Princeton, New Jersey : Princeton University Press, [2017] |
    Series: Lives of great religious books | Includes bibliographical
    references and index.
Identifiers: LCCN 2016045969
ISBN 9780691155586 (hardcover : alk. paper)
Subjects: LCSH: Qur'an—Translations into English—History and
    criticism.
Classification: LCC BP131.15.E54 L39 2017 | DDC 297.1/225—dc23
    LC record available at https://lccn.loc.gov/2016045969

British Library Cataloging-in-Publication Data is available

This book has been composed in Garamond Premier Pro

Printed on acid-free paper. ∞

Printed in the United States of America

10 9 8 7 6 5 4 3 2 1

To James Kritzeck (1930–1986)

CONTENTS

To translate or not to translate? When the text in question is the Arabic Qur'an there has always been hesitation, reluctance, and even resistance to translate. In English Qur'an became Anglicized as *Koran*, and since the eighteenth century *Koran* has supplanted all other options as the most frequently used substitute for Qur'an in Euro-American circles.[1] Yet *the Koran* did not, and for some it cannot, replace *the* Qur'an; only the latter, the Arabic Qur'an, is deemed to be the Word of God, the Noble Book, disclosed in the seventh century of the Common Era. At once holy and ancient, it was said to be revealed directly from the divine source, Allah, via a celestial intermediary, the Archangel Gabriel, to a human receptor, the Arab prophet Muhammad. Of itself, it says:

> *A Book whose signs have been distinguished*
> *as an Arabic Koran for a people having knowledge.*
>   Q 41:3[2]

Or sometimes it simply refers to itself as the *Koran*, as in:

> *Y. S. By the Koran, which is full of wisdom*
>   Q 36:1–2[3]

The truth of Islam as a revealed religion rests on a double axis. It is predicated *both* on prophecy as a divinely initiated process *and* its finality in the person of Muhammad: he was the last prophet who received the last revelation as *signs* (with Arabic, *ayat*, also meaning "verses") in the form of an Arabic Qur'an. The Arabic Qur'an then becomes more than law or guidance or even a sacred book; it is also disclosure of the Divine Will for all humankind in all places at all times. Arabic becomes not just one among many languages but the key index to salvation, prioritized over any other human language.

History versus Orthodoxy

Does the priority of Arabic then preclude the transmission of the Qur'anic message in languages other than Arabic? The orthodox view is yes; only in Arabic is the Qur'an truly the Qur'an. Arabic was the language of the final revelation, and the Arabic text remains untranslatable. Yet not all those who later heard the Arabic Qur'an were Arabs or knew Arabic. As Islam spread and many non-Arabs became Muslims, translations, mostly interlinear insertions in the Arabic text, did occur, but they remained few.[4] Only recently have translations proliferated, especially in English.

This staggered process raises a number of further questions: Is the Qur'an to be judged on the anvil of history, where translation intrudes and recurs? Or must the revealed text always be distilled through a filter of orthodoxy, privileging pristine Arabic and avoiding or degrading other languages? To grasp its message, does one elevate seventh-century Arabic, and by extension Arab origins, across time and space? What of the many Muslims, the majority of a 1.5-billion-person community, who are non-Arab and unacquainted with Arabic, save through the Qur'an?

Again and again one must ask: which predominates, the anvil of history or the filter of orthodoxy? There is no single, easy answer. Use of *Koran* rather than Qur'an is itself a choice of history over orthodoxy; despite the usage of centuries, from the twelfth to the twenty-first, of the name *Koran*, the orthodox would still say that any reference in any language to the Noble Book, the Word of God in Arabic, must be Qur'an or al-Qur'an. Beyond the Qur'an/*Koran* choice, the same query applies to the entirety of the Noble Book and to all texts, sacred and profane, that are translated: can any text be translated without sacrifice of the original meaning, and once translated, who judges whether that sacrifice is warranted, the outcome justified, the product edifying?

These queries about translation seemed novel to me in spring 1961. It was then that I took a course on Russian literature in translation at Princeton University. The lecturer was a European literary critic, George Steiner. Focusing on the limits of memory, Steiner lamented the lack of any means to assess a hierarchy of value. In the mind of every translator, according to Steiner, there exists a hierarchy of value among languages. How do these linguistic registers interact in the mind of each person who undertakes to translate, whether he or she is bilingual, trilingual, or multilingual?

The clue is to be found in the Tower of Babel. It was the image of this chaotic space and experience that gave Steiner the title for his classic study: *After Babel: Aspects of Language and Translation* (1975). The Tower of Babel is itself open to opposite interpretations. Many focus on the disaster of Babel. It prefigures the scattering of languages, tribes, and cultures that has led to endless strife and destructive, even cataclysmic warfare. Yet there is another view that favors rather than laments linguistic polyphony. Could one not argue that through the Tower of Babel, and because of the Tower of Babel, the God of the Torah, the Bible, and the Qur'an—the One who is also Omniscient Creator, the Lord of History and Destiny—has decreed that there be many languages? Might there not be a Divine basis for the healthy diversity of expressiveness that binds as well as divides humankind? Even Holy Writ is ambiguous. The book of Genesis declares: "It was called Babel—because there the Lord confused the language of the whole world. From there the Lord scattered them over the face of the whole earth" (Genesis 11:9). And the Qur'an makes an even stronger claim when it declares:

> *And among the signs of God*
> *is the creation of the heavens and the earth,*
> *and the diversity of your languages and colors.*
> *Surely in that are signs for those who know.*
>   Q 30:22[5]

Let us suppose that there is not just divinely intended linguistic confusion, as the Bible hints, but also divinely decreed diversity, as the Qur'an declares. Might not the benefit of linguistic diversity then hinge on avoiding literalism? For when translators claim to be literalists, they follow a principle that is inherently hierarchical and reductionist. They privilege one word and its meaning above any other option. They view multiple meanings as impossible. They reject every plurality as at once a distraction and a digression from the perfect original. The original must remain untranslated, or if translated, it must be singular, word-for-word, above challenge or change. "Such translators claim to adhere to a word-for-word technique in the name of ideal penetration," observes Steiner, "of a submission to the original so manifest and humble that it will elicit the entirety of meaning intact.... The translator does not aim to appropriate and bring home 'new' meaning. He seeks to remain 'inside' the source. He deems himself no more than a transcriber."[6]

In approaching translation of the *Koran* into English, the Italians, or at least some Italians, come down in favor of literalism. A famous Italian saying plays on the words "translation" and "betrayal": *Traduttore traditore*. Literally, it means "translator traitor." That is to say, every translator is a traitor. S/he betrays two languages, the original language of the source text, and also the other language of the receiving or target community. Translation, it seems, is always a lose-lose contest. The beauty of the original is lost, the meaning in the secondary version, even in the best word-to-word equivalence, becomes inchoate—reductive at best, inaccurate at worst, lost in every instance.[7]

And so one must consider a stark choice: is the Tower of Babel ugly or beautiful, dooming or ennobling? I have long asked these questions, nowhere more often than when surveying efforts to understand the *Koran* in English. The debate about the benefit, or liability, of translation impacts all efforts to render the Arabic Qur'an into any language, whether Persian or Turkish, Latin or English. The Italian case has been made anew by Stefan Wild, a preeminent German scholar. "No translation of any text from any language into another language," laments Wild, "can hope to give more than a translation of the meaning of the text; the rest is usually lost in translation. And *it is beyond dispute* that a word in LANGUAGE A can never correspond completely to a similar word or a word with the same meaning in LANGUAGE B."

The Qur'an is said to retain rhetorical features akin to verse, even while the orthodox claim it is not poetry.[8] Wild straddles that barrier of ambivalence through the famous ninth-century Arab humanist, al-Jāḥiẓ. Wild cites al-Jāḥiẓ in order to underscore how the Qur'an is like poetry even without being categorized as such. "Arabic poetry is untranslatable," al-Jāḥiẓ has argued; "it cannot be adapted to any other language. When this is attempted its structure is shattered, its metre is destroyed, its beauty disappears, and its marvels fall away." And so, concludes Wild, we face a similar problem in approaching the Arabic Qur'an. "The miraculous rhetorical quality that the Qur'anic text (in Arabic) has for the believer does defy translation."[9]

Believers, like scholars, often shore up the superiority as well as the untranslatability of the Arabic Qur'an. Murad Hofmann, a prominent German convert to Islam, echoes the argument and the sentiment of Wild when he declares: "Only the Arabic text of the Qur'an deserves the name 'Qur'an.' Muslims always knew that translating it, no matter into which language, is highly problematic since translations willy nilly are interpretations which cannot help reducing the semantic richness of the original."[10]

The argument advanced by Wild, Hofmann, and a host of others is most easily grasped in a three-step syllogism: If you don't know Arabic, you cannot understand the Qur'an. Without understanding the Qur'an, you cannot become a Muslim. Unless you become a Muslim, you cannot be saved. Therefore, you must know Arabic to be saved.

Most non-Muslims would disagree. Among them are some leading Christian scholars who have argued for making the Qur'an available in a European language. The earliest effort came in the twelfth century from an Englishman working in Spain. Robert of Ketton produced a remarkable translation of the Qur'an into Latin. It had few successors, yet the Swiss reformer Theodore Bibliander reproduced Robert's Qur'an in his own sixteenth-century edition, commended by no less a figure than Martin Luther. Luther's motives were mixed; though he feared the Muslim infidel, Luther recognized the appeal of scripture, Qur'anic as well as biblical. He did not want to refute the Qur'an so much as to assure his fellow Christians of the superiority of Christ over Muhammad and Christianity over Islam. To that end he urged his flock "to read the writings of the enemy."[11]

Few Christians shared Luther's enthusiasm to know the Qur'an in Latin, or in any European language. It was not until the eighteenth century that Robert's successors began to translate the *Koran* into English.[12] Muslims waited still longer. Not until the dawn of the twentieth century did Muslims undertake *Koran* translations, and then it was not Arabic-speaking Muslims but Muslims living in the Asian subcontinent who accepted the challenge; insistently and repeatedly, Indian Muslims tried to render the Noble Book into English, albeit with conflicting strategies.[13]

What all translators—Muslim or Christian, Asian or European—faced was orthodox reluctance to grant any *conceptual* benefit to the target language. The most one could achieve was a loose interpretation, a distant gloss of the pristine, original Book in Arabic. It was, after all, a Divine Text at once unassailable in meaning and untranslatable in practice.

Salvation beyond Prophecy?

Faced with the recurrent claim of Arabic exceptionalism, one must ask: does the Qur'an itself make such a sweeping claim of its own fortress-like separation from, and above, all other languages? Yes, the Qur'an was disclosed in Arabic to an Arab prophet in the seventh century, but it also proclaimed its message as eternally valid—valid for all who preceded Muhammad, most of whom did not speak Arabic, and also for all who would come after him, the majority of whom also were non-Arab. Indeed, few Muslims, less than 20 percent of all Muslims, were—or are—native speakers of Arabic. Is the Qur'anic message then restricted only to those who acknowledge prophets and also know Arabic?

It is noteworthy that the spiritual giant, Maulana Jalaluddin Rumi (d. 1273), founder of the whirling dervishes and author of poetry still recited throughout the Muslim world, echoed a deep élan for linguistic pluralism when he observed: "God's treasure houses are many, and God's knowledge is vast. If a man reads *one Koran* knowledgeably, why should he reject any *other Koran*? . . . In the time of Moses, Jesus, and others the *Koran* existed; that is, God's Word existed; it simply wasn't in Arabic."[14]

Rumi's plea is expansionist, but underlying it is the presumed superiority of prophecy—in some language, whether Arabic or another—and the restriction of salvation to those who acknowledge prophets. The Qur'an seems to agree. Q 5 "The Table" provides a decree supporting law as well as prophecy. It comes from the agent for disclosing the Divine message to the Prophet Muhammad, the Archangel Gabriel. After describing how Law or Torah had come to Jews and Law as Gospel to Christians, offering guidance and admonition for both, the Archangel Gabriel announces to Muhammad:

> For each of them We have established a law,
> and a revealed way.

And if God had wished,
He would have made you a single nation;
but the intent is to test you
in what He has given you.
So compete with one another
in good deeds.
Your destiny, everyone, is to God,
Who will tell you about
that wherein you differed.

Q 5:48[15]

This is good news, but only for the devout few—Jews, Christians, and Muslims—who believe in prophecy, in whatever language their prophet speaks. Is there then no hope for those who do not acknowledge prophecy, that is, those other than Jews, Christians, and Muslims who do not believe in prophets? They may have laws, but are such laws effective for the next life if they are not based on prophecy or relating to prophets?

On this point the Qur'an is equivocal: it implies that the only differences that matter are among those who have acknowledged both law and revelation ("a revealed way"). The rest of humanity seems to be passed over in silence. At least one noted Muslim historian, however, argues for a broader frame of possibility. A North African jurist, Ibn Khaldun, authored the *Muqaddimah* at the end of the fourteenth century. His work, a landmark of Islamic historiography, included this challenging observation: "People who have a (divinely revealed) book and who follow the prophets are few in number in comparison with the Magians who have none. The latter constitute the majority of the world's inhabitants."[16]

And who created the majority of the world's inhabitants if not the same God, the God of Abraham, Isaac, Jacob, Jesus, and Muhammad? At the outset of the twenty-first century, there are still more Magians than muslims, despite missionary initiatives and conversion efforts that have intensified during the past 150 years, especially in Africa.[17] And so Ibn Khaldun's larger point is worth pondering: did the One, the Absolute, the Other not have a design for the pagan many as well as for the pious few, at all times and in all places? While belief/ unbelief may be crucial theological criteria, they are human reflexes, and do they exhaust the limits of Divine mercy? Pluralists would argue that our deepest mandate is to seek the Divine intent in *every* family of the human race, not just in the Abrahamic subset, those privileged by prophecy. Equally urgent is the mandate to seek traces of Divine splendor in *every* extant language, not just in Qur'anic Arabic but in every post-Babel tongue of humankind.

This is the minority view, however. Through the filter of orthodoxy, which dominates, the emphasis shifts from all humankind to one subset. It is not the many Magians but the few muslims, whether they be devoted to the Prophet and observant of the Qur'an or merely following some other Law and Revealed Way, it is they, and they alone, who are privileged with hope, mercy, and good fortune on the Day of Judgment. And their destiny is wrapped up in one language, the Arabic Qur'an:

And We have revealed it as an Arabic Qur'an
that you [people who accept prophets] *might understand.*
    Q 12:2[18]

The Evidence of Practice

It could be argued, however, that the skein of prophecy itself has been expanded through the latest chapter in the saga of Babel and its Tower. In 2017, there is more to the Qur'an than the Arabic Qur'an. Arabic to English is no longer a mere option; it is a pervasive reality. Whether as problem or prospect, challenge or opportunity, the Arabic Qur'an has been rendered into the English *Koran* multiple times. Halting at first, this process has now accelerated beyond what any could have imagined at the turn of the twentieth century. During the past century English translations of the *Koran* proliferated. They numbered sixty. Is that a lot? Yes, but the total pales in comparison to what lies ahead. Although the twenty-first century has yet to complete its second decade the number of complete translations of the *Koran* into English has soared; in 2017 its total has already reached forty-five.

The acceleration of *Koran*s in English is even more startling when one compares rates. In the entire twentieth century there was about one translation every other year, but even less if one discounts rank plagiarisms. By contrast, in a little more than fifteen years, the twenty-first century has been witnessing almost three new translations every year, most original and several available online.[19]

It is no longer a question of whether but how, and how well, the Arabic Qur'an will become the *Koran* in English. Rumi's advice needs to be repeated and expanded: the *Koran* can be read in some language other than Arabic, not just by generations past but also by generations still to come. The horse has bolted from the stable; the gate cannot be closed. History has lurched forward to this threshold, with its resounding dictum: the fate of the Arabic Qur'an is not exceptional, either in the annals of world literature or on the spectrum of world religions. Recourse to English translations, both online and offline, has become ubiquitous in the twenty-first century. The *Koran* in English will expand and expand, becoming more rather than less influential during this century and beyond.

The Ahmadi Challenge

History is a beacon to the future. What has made the Qur'an exceptional is not its literary past but its historical trajectory. Crucial is empire, specifically the fate of Muslim empires during the past four centuries. European conquest led to Christian rule over African and Asian domains with major Muslim populations. Ottomans, Safavids, and Mughals—all experienced the fate of Euro-American ascendance. That process, begun in the sixteenth century, accelerated in the nineteenth century with missionary activity throughout the colonial possessions of the British and the French (and to a much lesser extent Italians, Dutch, Germans, as well as Russians) prior to World War I.

Protestant missionaries, including Americans by the end of the nineteenth century, disseminated the Bible in multiple languages, but the British took the lead in mandating English as the dominant language of public exchange.

It is impossible to overstate the pervasive presence of British soldiers and administrators, institutions and values in what is now known as the Indian subcontinent. Their dependence on English was shared by their subjects. Much has been written of this period and this process, but one understudied aspect was the impact of English as a scriptural language on those indigenous elites, Muslim, Hindu, Sikh, and Buddhist, who knew English but were not Christian.

A delayed response to the challenge of biblical English was the *Koran* in English. The *Koran* itself, as noted above, is shorthand for a larger process. The very name *Koran* was a translation of al-Qur'an, the Arabic Qur'an. Every published *Koran* valorized the endeavor to translate the Arabic Qur'an into English. Often it was not translated directly but instead via Persian or Urdu into English since it was Indian Muslims who were most intent on producing their equivalent, their "answer," to the English Bible. Crucial intermediaries for this two-stage process of translation were Indian Muslims who were neither Sunni nor Shiʿi but Ahmadi. Ahmadi Muslims are a tiny offshoot of Sunni Islam, yet it is they who produced the earliest *Muslim* translations of the Qur'an into French and German as well as English.

To date, few have examined, or tried to understand, the pervasive impact of Ahmadi *Koran* translations. Ahmadi linguists spurred intense effort, especially among their South Asian Sunni counterparts, to produce comparable and—so their followers have claimed—superior English translations. Yet today the pioneering Ahmadi translations have been universally marginalized; Sunni Muslim opponents revile the approach of their Ahmadi precursors, no matter how pious their intent, how competent their product.

These brief observations raise a further query: Why has *intra*-Muslim competition fueled rival translations? Orthodoxy, Sunni defined orthodoxy, has required major scholars to establish a criterion that places Ahmadis outside the circle of Muslim translators. It was not always so. In the 1930s Abdullah Yusuf Ali, born a Bohra or Shi'i Muslim, embraced Sunni loyalties and emerged as arguably the foremost translator of the *Koran* into English. He commended his Muslim predecessors in the preface to his 1937 translation.[20] He does demarcate Muslim from non-Muslim efforts, but while citing the mischief of the latter to explain the motive of the former, Yusuf Ali includes the Ahmadis among his Muslim predecessors. Other Sunni Muslims have not followed his lead. Recently, Abdur Raheem Kidwai published a capacious review of sixty English translations of the *Koran*. Even while applauding the early twentieth-century Sunni translators, especially Abdullah Yusuf Ali and Marmaduke Pickthall, Kidwai rank orders all translations according to their qualities as "orthodox," with the Ahmadis ranked lower than others; they are singled out for repeated, severe criticism.[21]

The standard of orthodoxy shifts, however, from author to author. There is no uniform or consensus taxonomy. Each evaluator reveals different criteria. Online, the webmaster deems all to be equally valid or else ranks entries, but without criteria. Offline, the translator(s) must plead honesty and often provide some criteria for measuring excellence. While I will examine several translation initiatives, many undertaken with great sacrifice as well as dogged personal commitment, it is crucial to note that most efforts to evaluate the *Koran* in English are made online by nontranslators. Not just the Ahmadis but also those pre-twentieth-century translators classified as Orientalists are uniformly debunked in the reflexively orthodox gaze that prevails online.

These same translators look very different when revisited offline and in the light of history. Examining their actual labor, one can see an enormous internal diversity. No less devout than their "orthodox" counterparts, what they have made of the Arabic Qur'an in modern English more often engages and defends, rather than defames and ridicules, the revelations delivered to Muhammad in the seventh century. Not all translations were done in bad faith, and even non-Muslim adversaries of Islam often found in al-Qur'an a rich source of insight into the universe as well as humankind.

An Overview

The chapters that follow will trace the ongoing battle over the *Koran* as an English stepchild or linguistic equivalent of al-Qur'an, its Arabic original. After etching the main features of the Prophet as transmitter of revelation in chapter one, I explore a range of contestants from several regions and multiple languages, Latin, French, and German as well as English, from the eleventh to the nineteenth centuries, in chapter two. By the early decades of the twentieth century the stakes in *Koran* translation had mushroomed, especially in South Asia, and chapter three traces the Ahmadi impact on subsequent developments that affect English translations throughout the twentieth century. Chapter four brings the contest up to the year 2017. It examines the millennial generation, custodians of the virtual era that began with the Internet in 1994. Twenty years later we now need to survey the impact of the Internet on the diversity of English translations; despite its popularity and widespread acceptance, major gaps, in information but also interpretation, undermine the reliability of the World Wide Web as a ready resource for *Koran* translations.

Chapter five highlights actual differences in translations, drawing on both full and partial translations of crucial Qur'anic passages. Since few sacred texts are exempt from institutional influence and/or manipulations, chapter six explores the politics of *Koran* translation, from Arabia to America, looking at how and why certain translations have been favored and promoted over others. Chapter seven takes an unexpected turn. It introduces *American Qur'an*, produced by California artist Sandow Birk. Best understood as the Graphic *Koran*, Birk's masterpiece[22] is a product of 9/11 that invites its twenty-first-century audience to reconsider the legacy of Islam through reading the English *Koran* with background images from American life. At once ancient text and modern mirror, *American Qur'an* offers a new, bold threshold for cultural as well as literary translation. The conclusion weaves together several strands of commentary and criticism projecting a way forward for the *Koran* in English.

LIVES OF GREAT RELIGIOUS BOOKS

The *Koran* in English

Muhammad and Revelation

The Essentials

Any narrative about the Arabic Qur'an must begin in the seventh century, with the life of Muhammad ibn Abdullah, the Arab Prophet.[1] The Qur'an was revealed to this Arab merchant/trader through a celestial intermediary, the Archangel Gabriel, in his own language, Arabic. It was in Arabic, and solely in Arabic, that each of the Qur'an's 6,236 verses and 114 chapters was announced to Muhammad.[2] Biography and revelation are intertwined, so even to recount in English the story of the last prophet requires use of *Koran* translations; several are provided below.[3]

The sparsest outline of the life of Muhammad would include five dates: Born in 570 CE, he married in 595 CE, was called to prophesy in Mecca in 610 CE, then left Mecca for Yathrib/Medina in 622 CE, and after subduing his enemies, died in Medina in 632 CE at the age of sixty-two.

But the impress of the Qur'an in Muhammad's life demands more. It requires beginning with his early life. For the first forty years Muhammad was an orphan, raised by his uncle, with his first cousin 'Ali as a companion. He later became a merchant, traveling beyond Arabia but always returning to Mecca. He only became a messenger under duress. The message was not his own, nor did he seek it. The message sought him, filled him and transformed him, making his life a journey that none, including he, could have imagined.

Before Revelation

Muhammad was a successful merchant but a reluctant messenger. His success at the business owned by his wife, Khadija, allowed him time to reflect. Like others in his community, he set aside time to go to a mountain, to a mountain cave. Between caravan trips that took him away from home to places near and far, he would stay at home but in a place apart. He would go to this mountain retreat often. Sometimes he would go there by himself or with his young cousin. He would sit quietly and ponder what life means.

What does it mean that he was born an orphan but found a new family among his close relatives? What does it mean that he had been an honest but poor merchant until a wealthy widow found him, employed him, trusted him, and then married him?

Although he felt gratitude for the gifts of family and wealth, he still lacked something. It was that lack that drove him to the mountain retreat, to find a space within himself and apart from others—except for his young cousin 'Ali—to ponder the mystery of human success and the lessons of human failure.

Like many of his tribe, he had acknowledged the power of the rock that marked his home town of Mecca. The Ka'ba contained that rock, a rock ancient with history. It is linked to an early seeker of Truth, a prophet in his time, named Abraham. It was to this place that Abraham sent his concubine Hagar. It is here that Abraham, with divine guidance, made provision for a branch of his family, and its central role has been etched in the Qur'an:

> *Our Lord* [prayed Abraham] *I have settled*
> *some of my children*
> *in a barren valley*
> *near Your Holy House,*
> *our Lord,*
> *that they may be constant in prayer,*
> *making the hearts of some incline to them*
> *and providing them with fruit,*
> *that they may give thanks.*
> Q 14:37[4]

But the Holy House became a place that Abraham shared with others, with idols that represented local gods and tribal deities. These idols were said to possess a power that rivaled the God of Abraham. Some folk who came to Mecca cast doubt on the power of the idols, saying that after Abraham came other seekers of Truth, other prophets, each proclaiming a god not found in idols. Some opponents of the idols were the Jews. Their prophet was Moses. Other opponents were the Christians. Their prophet was Jesus, though some of them went further, claiming that Jesus was more than a prophet. Muhammad also met some Arab opponents of idol worship. They claimed that there was an ancient Arab prophet, Salih by name, and that he too followed the way of Moses and Jesus, looking for the source of all life and all created forms, beyond idols of any shape or any place. It was Salih who said to his people what was later revealed to Muhammad:

> *O my people, serve God.*
> *You have no god except Him.*
> *It is He who raised you from the earth*
> *and settled you in it.*
> *Seek His forgiveness,*
> *then turn to Him in repentance.*
> *My Lord is Near, Responsive.*
>   Q 11:61[5]

Muhammad meditated on these matters when he sat in the cave of Hira during the holy month of Ramadan. Ramadan was the time each year when blood feuds were suspended. It was a time when Meccans who had wealth and free time could retreat to the outskirts of their town, to the hills that enclosed it, and to the caves that offered shelter and repose.

Revelation

Muhammad had been following the practice of retreat and meditation for over a decade. Then one night in

Ramadan 610 he felt a stirring inside him. He loved the nighttime in this special month; it drew him deep into himself and allowed him to resist those impulses that pulled him back to the world, to concerns with family or with business or travel. He was alert to repel those impulses. They clouded his vision, they denied him peace of mind, but above all, they blocked his search for the Truth. But this was a different stirring. It was deep, it was arresting. It overpowered him, and then it produced words, words that were not his. He listened:

"Recite!" And he was shown a piece of silk with words on it.

He did not know how to read. "What shall I recite?" he asked.

"Recite!" came the command, and again the brocade was thrust before him.

He stammered: "But what shall I recite?"

He became like the Prophet Jeremiah who was told by the Lord of Israel to speak when he was a child and he could not. Unlike Jeremiah, Muhammad could speak but he could not read. All those who accompanied him on caravan trips, whether to Egypt or Syria, to Yemen or Abyssinia, knew that he could read symbols but not words. It was they who handled the few documents of exchange that required reading or signing. When Muhammad had to sign, he would ask others to read aloud what was written, then he would sign by pressing the palm of his hand to the paper. Why then did this voice ask him to recite?

Even as he was thinking these thoughts, for the third time, the voice commanded him:

"Recite!"

"But what, what shall I recite?"

No sooner had he spoken than the words appeared:

Recite in the name of your Lord who created
Created man from blood coagulated
Recite for your Lord is Most Generous
Who taught by the pen
Taught what they did not know unto men
   Q 96:1–5[6]

These words became part of him. He recited them without reading them. But why did they invoke the Lord as *His* Lord? And why did they rhyme? "Created" rhymed with "coagulated" in the first two lines, and then "pen" with "men" in the fourth and fifth lines. Since Muhammad could not read the words, he was puzzled, dismayed. Had it been his secret impulses that had produced these verses? Had he become a man possessed, an ecstatic poet such as his clansmen distrusted, even despised? Was his pursuit of the Truth forfeited by a single moment of self-deceit?

Scarcely had he absorbed the experience when his whole body began to tremble. Then the voice spoke again. It addressed him by name: "O Muhammad!" "Muhammad," it continued, "you cannot protect yourself from the Evil One. Only the One who hears all and knows all can protect you. Invoke God but before you mention God by His loftiest name, say 'I seek refuge from Satan, the Accursed, in the name of the One who hears all and knows all.' Before you repeat the words I have just given you from

Your Lord, say: 'In the name of God, Full of Compassion, Ever Compassionate!'" and the silence descended.

He waited for more counsel. He needed advice. What was he to do? Where should he go? How was he to make sense of all this? But nothing more came. In a flash, he got up and bolted down the mountain, running toward Mecca, toward home, toward Khadija, his beloved wife. Halfway down the voice returned. Now it was a booming voice with a face, a man's face. The face appeared to come from beyond the horizon. The celestial form announced: "O Muhammad, you are the apostle of God, and I am Gabriel." He tried to look away but wherever he looked, there was the face; there was the man, staring at him.

He could not move. He was frozen on that spot. For the longest time he stood there, until finally his wife, Khadija, sent scouts to look for him. They found him. They brought him home. As soon as they left he collapsed into his wife's lap. He told her what had happened on this strangest of days atop Mount Hira. "O son of my uncle," she exclaimed, addressing him with the same name that she had when she had proposed marriage to him some fifteen years earlier, "O son of my uncle, be at ease and rejoice. In the name of the One who enfolds the soul of Khadija, I can dare to hope that you have been chosen to be the prophet for this people."

A prophet for his people?! How could a mere merchant attuned to meditative silence become a messenger who must proclaim the message, often against his own deep wishes and even more, against the preferences and practices of his people? Every prophet, after all, is also a rebel. Muhammad had never seen himself in this role. Nothing in his life had prepared him for the period of trial that now beset him. His wife and also his young cousin came to view him in a different light. He was still their close companion, but now they saw him as one separate, apart, more respected than loved, though always cared for, his words and wishes heeded. Yet others were less kind, even rude, often taunting him for his "poetic" outbursts, his "pretended" inspiration.

And so Muhammad had to wrestle with a double doubt. Could he be worthy of this high calling? And if he were, then why did this voice that came to him not come more often and more insistently? He had long periods when there would be no inner voice. Whenever he did hear that voice, he would repeat what he heard so that others could remember the exact words. Above all, he depended on his beloved and trusting wife, Khadija. She became the first Muslim, a woman to honor all women and to make them companion believers with men. And after her came his young cousin, that boy 'Ali, who was so quick and constant in his affection for Muhammad.

The Night Journey

The most difficult time happened in 617. He had received many communications from beyond. Although the fear of being a possessed seer or ecstatic poet had passed, he lived every hour in the shadow of that protective phrase known as the *basmala*: "In the Name of God,

Full of Compassion, Ever Compassionate." Each time the voice spoke, he repeated these words to make sure that it was indeed the Lord of Life who was speaking to him, not the Accursed one, Satan slinking into his mind, whispering in the garb of God.

Yet even the *basmala* could not overcome the hostility of some in his town. The most trying experience came in the middle of a night during that year 617. Many of his clansmen and fellow Arabs had come to accept his new status as an apostle among them. Yet the more popular he became, the louder were his detractors. One day he had suffered more abuse than even he could bear. At night, in despair he had called out to the voice, and to the Lord of Life. He had begged for some sign that he might endure and, if God willed, that he might prevail against his adversaries. What happened next was both vivid and unspeakable. In the words of a poet:

> He came to me, wrapped in the cloak of night,
> Approaching with steps of caution and fright.
> Then what happened, happened; to say more fails.
> Imagine the best; ask not for details.[7]

Details cannot convey what did happen on that night. And though some have argued about whether it was a physical or a "mere" dreamlike experience, the impact was beyond dispute.[8] It reminded Muhammad of that first night, the night of Ramadan when Gabriel had come to him as a voice, as a face, as a presence that could not be denied. Later it had been revealed to him that that first night was to be the Great Sign containing even as it unfolded all that followed. It was the Night of Destiny, revealed in the Noble Qur'an:

We have sent it down in the Night of Destiny
What will unmask for you the Night of Destiny?
The single Night of Destiny
Is better than a thousand months.
In it angels and the spirit alight,
On every errand by God made right
Peace reigns until dawn's early light.
    Q 97[9]

Seven years later the Night Journey followed that Night of Destiny. Both nights were shrouded in mystery, yet they contain and define the life of Muhammad more vividly than did any daytime event. It seemed as though a mere instant separated one from the other, or was it perhaps time itself that had been transformed by the Unseen? While the Night of Destiny had brought the majesty of heaven to earth and to an unsuspecting messenger, the Night Journey propelled him to another place and finally to a celestial destination. The Night Journey took Muhammad from Mecca to Jerusalem to the highest throne of heaven. The same voice announced what was to happen. It was the now familiar voice, the voice of Gabriel. It beckoned Muhammad to ascend to the Source of all Truth and Life, the Touchstone of Peace and Justice:

By the star when it sets,
Your companion neither worries nor frets
Nor does he ever speak with regrets.

It is only revelation that he begets,
It is One mighty in power who projects,
And propels him upward to what perfects,
Far beyond the horizon where the sun sets,
Nearer and nearer to the source he trajects,
So close that a mere bowline between them intersects.
    Q 53:1–9[10]

With these words from the Star chapter, Muhammad was transported on a winged horse to the rock where Abraham nearly sacrificed his son Ishmael. It was a great rock in an ancient city, Jerusalem. Jerusalem was the abode of prophets, from Abraham to David to Jesus. And it now hosted another prophet, the Arab prophet, the Prophet Muhammad. Dazzled, he was transported from that rock up to heaven. Heaven had levels. At the first level many angels and the prophet Adam greeted him. At the second level of heaven it was other prophets, Jesus and John the Baptist, who hailed him. At the third level he met still other prophets, Joseph and Solomon, and at the fourth level he encountered Moses along with Mary, the mother of Jesus. Now his glorious steed seemed to fade. Yet he continued to progress upward. "It is One mighty in power who projects." Arriving at the fifth level, he met the prophets Ishmael and Isaac, then the prophets Elijah and Noah at the sixth, until finally at the seventh level he was dazzled by yet another chorus of angels. In their midst was the greatest of prophets, the Prophet Abraham. Abraham greeted Muhammad warmly before sending him on to the Divine Throne.

At last, no more than a bowline seemed to intersect between Muhammad and the Glorious and Exalted One. Gabriel spoke on His behalf. He offered Muhammad and his community protection if they would but pray fifty times per day. Muhammad nodded and retreated. But as he began to return to earth Moses reminded him that fifty prayers were too many for his Arab followers. Muhammad returned. He requested a reduced protocol of piety. Gabriel became his arbiter. Twenty-five prayers? Ten prayers? Finally, Muhammad was granted a divine reprieve: from that day until the Day of Resurrection, incumbent on him and all his followers was the daily recital of five prayers. A mere five times of prayerful remembrance had to punctuate each day with thoughts and desires directed solely to the Lofty One.

And then it was over. Muhammad descended by the same celestial route that he had ascended. He returned to the Temple Mount in Jerusalem from where he had begun his ascent, and in the twinkle of an eye he was back in Mecca. The next morning Muhammad awoke still stunned by the Night Journey yet comforted, his confidence restored.

Last Years in Mecca

He needed confidence to face the many trials that were to beset him in Mecca. One trial was perhaps the most painful. It occurred right after the Night Journey. It was as though the Compassionate One had wanted to be certain that Muhammad not take pride in his own role as messenger. Even though he was the one chosen to repeat God's message of what God was to all Arabs, and to all humankind, he was still a mortal, a mere man like other men.

In the very same Star chapter (Q 53) Muhammad was chided about those gods of the Ka'ba that his tribe had worshiped before the Lord of the Ka'ba had called them to look beyond these idols, and to reject their intercessory power.

Have you then considered Lat and Uzza,
And another, the third, Manat?
Are the males for you and the females for Him?

Were these rhetorical questions, or was this an invitation to reconsider the intercessory power of the three idols? Muhammad may have hesitated, but the divine answer came in the next sweep of revelation:

This is indeed an unfair division!
They are only names that you yourself have named,
You and your father; God has not granted them a position.
They follow but fancy and what their lower selves requisition
It is only from their Lord that they find guidance and
*   decision.*
Does man get whatever he hankers for?
No, all that has gone before and all that comes after
This life belongs only to the Lord of Life, to God!
*   Q 53:19–25*[11]

Since that first revelation on Mount Hira some seven years previous, Muhammad had never felt so close to the line of distinction between what came to him from Above and from Below. Very early he had heard words that sounded like a talisman, an amulet to ease his troubled soul. They were words that he repeated often when he felt the need for divine protection from other words, other whisperings that were not from Above but from Below:

In the name of God Full of Compassion, Ever
    Compassionate
Repeat: I seek protection with the Lord of Creation
the King of Creation
the God of Creation
From the malicious incantations
Of the Accursed, whispering insinuations
In the hearts of jinn and humankind both, fabrications.
    Q 114[12]

What were these staccato-like phrases if not a divine incantation? Muhammad felt their power, and their comfort, especially when he was confronted not just with disbelievers but also with rival messengers. One such was Musaylima, who claimed the power to counter ambivalent spirits (*jinn*) and, above all, the least ambivalent and most lethal of spirits, Satan. Musaylima identified himself as an apostle of the One beyond all comparison, even sometimes calling him the One Full of Compassion (*rahman*). And what was the "proof" of his prophecy? Rhymed prose utterances such as those Gabriel revealed to Muhammad.

But had either Musaylima or any other ever produced a message like the Qur'an? No, neither Musaylima nor any other so-called apostle could or did produce a book like this Qur'an in Arabic. Muhammad's people, like Jonah's people, were warned, not just about the Day of Judgment but also about false prophets. It is in the Jonah chapter that the Lofty One declares to Muhammad:

> *And this Qur'an is not something*
> *that could be manufactured without God;*
> *rather, it is a confirmation of what preceded it,*
> *and a clear explanation of the Book—*
> *there is no doubt in it—from the Lord of all creation.*
> *Do they perhaps say "He forged it"?*
> *Say, "Then bring a chapter like it,*
> *and call upon anyone other than God you can,*
> *if you are being truthful."*
>
> Q 10:37–38[13]

Because the Lord of all creation had revealed His Word to Muhammad, the prophet felt sustained against both doubters and imitators. He had been given not just the five daily prayers but also the creed, the alms for the poor, the fast of Ramadan, and the pilgrimage to the Lord of Ka'ba, all through this Book. The Book was an invitation, and it was also an opening of the Divine Abundance into the human domain, into the human heart. The Book itself announces the opening. The very first Sign is called the Opening chapter. It offers the gist, the fine gold dust, of All Revelations. It channels divine access through the Seven Portals of Hope, each of its seven verses marking a divine favor conferred on those who remember and those who recite these words. Collectively, the seven verses of the Opening chapter became

the gateway to spiritual health, for all believers, be they
Jews, Christians, or Muslims:

> *In the Name of God Full of Compassion, Ever*
>   *Compassionate*
> *Praise to the Lord of all Creation*
> *Full of Compassion, Ever Compassionate*
> *Master of the Day of Determination*
> *You alone do we worship*
> *And from You alone do we seek alleviation*
> *Guide us to the path of True Direction,*
> *The path of those whom You favor,*
> *Not of those who cause You indignation,*
> *Nor of those who took to the path of deviation.*
>   Q 1[14]

Vouchsafed by these words, by the intermittent an-
nouncements of Gabriel, by the salutary Signs from the
Unseen, Muhammad had begun his journey as a messenger of God. He had become a vehicle for the Unseen. At
the same time, for his enemies he remained a rebel against
his own people. He had reviled the Ka'ba; he had defiled
their native gods and traditions. By 618 his journey had
just begun. The orphan merchant had become an inspired messenger. Who could have imagined then where
this journey would take him during the next decade, for
the rest of his life, for the sweep of human history?

From the time of his first revelations Muhammad had
been buoyed with hope by his wife, Khadija, and also by
his uncle, Abu Talib. Khadija became the first Muslim,
and she comforted him from his first revelation until her

dying breath. Although Abu Talib did not become a Muslim, he still protected Muhammad. Not so another uncle, Abu Lahab, who confronted and tormented Muhammad. The raw opposition of this uncle dismayed him. Then there came to Muhammad as a further Sign from the Unseen that was also a counsel: to be a prophet he had to withstand such terrible men and women, for God would be his final protector.

> *In the Name of God Full of Compassion, Ever*
>   *Compassionate*
> *Abu Lahab and his power*
> *Both will expire.*
> *He will not be saved by wealth*
> *Or the profits he may acquire.*
> *He will be plunged*
> *Into lahab, a burning fire!*
> *And his wife—*
> *That kindling-carrier*
> *Will wear about her neck a halter of palm fibre!*
>   Q 111[15]

Death would be the great leveler: burning fire, hell fire awaited those who disobeyed God and heckled His Prophet. Yet despite the divine promise, death awaited not only Muhammad's foes, like Abu Lahab and his wife, but also those who were closest to Muhammad, his most intimate and trusted supporters. In 619 he endured what became the year of tragedy, *annus horribilus*, for him. In that same year he lost Khadija, his wife, his confidante, his mainstay in all that he did. He also lost Abu Talib, his uncle, his father by trust, his protector against hostile clansmen and other Meccan detractors. Without his protector at home and his shield beyond home, he became vulnerable to loneliness and to persecution.

The Exodus to Medina

Threatened by Meccan opponents, Muhammad sought help in other oases towns, with tribes beyond his own. He began to think the unthinkable, that he could not survive except at a distance from his native town and his tribesmen.

Muhammad's main channel of communication to the outside was through the annual fairs held on the outskirts of Mecca. It was a time when even his bitterest opponents could not assail him. More than commerce took place there. News about events in Arabia and beyond circulated at these fairs. At one such fair in 620 he met representatives from a tribe to the north. They met again the next year. They responded to the Qur'an, they accepted Islam, some had even begun to pray publicly on Friday. These were people from Yathrib, later known as the city of the Prophet or *Madinat al-nabi*, and today simply as Medina.

What a contrast to his native town! In Mecca the opposition to him and to his message continued to grow month by month. Muhammad had sent a group to Abyssinia earlier. They included his precious daughter, Ruqayya, and her husband, 'Uthman. They remained there protected by a generous and wise Christian king, but Muhammad needed another refuge within Arabia. The town to the north seemed like his best hope. He could go there but not without risking conflict with his neighbors and clansmen from Mecca. How could he take this step, even to save his own life? He could not take it except with help from the Unseen. The help came to him in a further Sign from God:

> *In the Name of God Full of Compassion, ever*
> *   Compassionate*
> *Permission to fight is given to those on whom war is made,*
> *because they are oppressed.*
> *And surely God is able to provide them victory*
> *(over their oppressors).*
> *Those who are driven from their homes without a just cause*
> *except that they say: Our Lord is God.*
> *And if God did not repel some people by others,*
> *Cloisters, and churches and synagogues, and mosques*
> *—in all of which God's name is remembered—*
> *All would have been pulled down.*
> *And surely God will help him who helps Him.*
> *Surely God is Strong and Mighty.*
>   Q 22: 39–40[16]

These precious verses provided the solace he sought, the command he needed, in order to flee with his closest supporters to the north, to Medina. There, with God's help, he could—and he did—begin a new life as the mediator of other groups' conflicts. At the same time, he continued to be the vessel of the Divine Word, the reciter of those blessed phrases that came from Beyond, from the

Archangel Gabriel. The year of his flight (*hijra*) was 622. The flight marked the beginning of a new moment, and also a new calendar; 622 became the first year for that community who accepted Muhammad, those who prayed with him, those who fought for his cause, those who, like him, waited for guidance from Beyond through Gabriel.

For Muhammad did not cease to be a reciter once he became a community advocate. He did not feel less the call of the Unseen. Now, though, he had to make choices as a military strategist. He had to defend his community against those who either betrayed or assaulted him. His enemies included some of the neighboring tribes, but all of them were connected to Mecca, either to his close relatives or to tribesmen. Among them were bitter foes, like his own uncle, Abu Lahab, whom God cursed through a revelation, along with his wife. Worst of all was the leader of the Makhzum clan of the Quraysh, Abu Jahl. Abu Jahl made a mockery of Muhammad and confronted his followers. Abu Jahl would single out converted slaves, and then have his hired thugs assault them. He would belittle in public or debar from markets other Meccan Muslims who may have been protected by family at home. He would also exclude them from caravan trips. He would harm them in any way he could.

Initial Wars

Once Muhammad was established in Medina he had no choice but to fight the likes of Abu Jahl. God Himself had declared: *"Permission to fight is given to those on whom war is made"* (Q 22.39). But it was always a defensive war, a reluctant recourse to violence when other stratagems had failed. The war Muhammad waged against Mecca was not a struggle for prestige or wealth; it was a war for the survival of God's Word. It was at the same time a war for personal survival. His helpers from Medina joined the migrants from Mecca. They provided the migrants with food and shelter from their own resources, but they were all stretched to the limit. They began to raid the caravans of their Meccan foes. They raided only small caravans at first, and never attacked during those times when fighting, especially blood feuds, were prohibited. As someone who had guided many a successful caravan to its destiny, Muhammad knew the routes. He knew the seasons. He also knew the wells where Meccan traders would pass with their camels and their goods.

In December 623, over a year after the beleaguered Muslims had fled to Medina, Muhammad ordered a small detachment to spy on a caravan to the south. It was proceeding along the route to Yemen, at the oasis of Nakhlah that links Mecca to Taif. It was the last day of the Holy Month of Rajab. He had ordered his followers not to attack but they disobeyed. They killed some, took others captive, and brought the caravan back to Medina.

Muhammad was appalled. Not only had his followers disobeyed him; they had also desecrated a holy month. They had gone against God's Word. Since their actions channeled his leadership, he was responsible. The prophet who had pledged to be a divine mediator had betrayed his own prophecy. He was riven with distress. He prayed to God. He needed guidance from above. And when it came, it was like a fresh rain after the longest, driest drought of summer:

> *They ask you about war in the holy month.*
> *Tell them:*
> *"To fight in that month is a great sin.*
> *But a greater sin in the eyes of God is*
> *to hinder people from the way of God,*
> *and not to believe in Him,*
> *and to bar access to the Holy Mosque,*
> *and to turn people out of its precincts.*
> *And oppression is worse than killing."*

He started to breathe a sigh of relief with these words, as the revelation continued:

> *They will always seek war against you*
> *till they turn you away from your faith,*
> *if they can.*
> *But those of you who turn back on their faith*
> *and die disbelieving*
> *will have wasted their deeds*
> *in this world and the next.*
> *They are inmates of Hell,*
> *and shall abide there forever.*
>   Q 2:217[17]

The Almighty had made possible what for men is impossible: a general rule of high value was replaced with a general rule of higher value. Yes, killing is forbidden in the sacred month, but worse than killing is oppression, hindering people from the way of God. Empowered by this Sign, Muhammad accepted the actions of his followers at Nakhlah. Taking the spoils of war, he divided them among all members of the community.

More war would follow. The provocation to his former tribesmen and townsmen was clearer than the desert sky. Muhammad and his followers braced for the next outbreak in what was to become an enduring conflict with their Meccan kinsmen and opponents. During the next nine years Muhammad planned thirty-eight battles that were fought by his fellow believers. He himself led twenty-seven military campaigns. The merchant messenger had become not only a recognized prophet but also a successful military strategist.

Muhammad did not have to wait long for the first full-scale military campaign that he led. It came at the wells of Badr the following year, in 624. It was less than four months after the skirmish at Nakhlah. The Muslims chose to attack a caravan coming south from Palestine to Mecca. The Meccans learned of their attack, opposing them with a force that far outnumbered the Muslim band. Muhammad and his followers should have lost; indeed, they would have lost, except for the intervention of angels. Appearing on their side was a heavenly host, a band of divine emissaries such as they had never seen before. The celestial warriors preceded their desert protégés. They watched over them. They bolstered them. They gained them a victory as the Almighty attested in yet another Sign:

God helped you during Badr
at a time when you were helpless,
So act in compliance with the laws of God:
You may well be grateful.
Remember when you said to the faithful:
"Is it not sufficient that your Lord
should send for your help
3,000 angels from the heavens?"
Indeed, if you are patient and take heed for yourselves,
even though the enemy come rushing at you suddenly,
your Lord will send 5,000 angels.
And God did not do so
but as good tidings for you,
and to reassure your hearts—
For victory comes from God alone,
the Almighty, the All-knowing.
    Q 3:123–26[18]

The Battle of Badr struck fear into the hearts of the Meccans, but it also made some even more firmly resolved to defeat the upstart Muslims. Among the Meccan opponents was Hind ibn Utbah, the wife of the mighty Meccan warrior Abu Sufyan. She had lost both her uncle and her father in the Battle of Badr. She incited her husband, though he was both Muhammad's cousin and his foster brother, to write verses against the Prophet and also against the religion of Islam. It was Abu Sufyan whose caravan the Muslims had tried to capture at the Battle of Badr. Although Muslims had won the battle, they lost the caravan. Soon after, Abu Sufyan, at his wife's insistence, began to plan for the next encounter. By 625 he had assembled a huge army of both foot soldiers and cavalry. He marched toward Medina. The Muslims countered by moving out of the city proper to engage their rivals on the slopes of a nearby mountain, Uhud.

Despite the superior numbers of the Meccans, it went well for the Muslims until some of Muhammad's followers broke ranks too early, perhaps anticipating another victory such as Badr. It was not to be. The Meccans counterattacked, and Khalid ibn al-Walid, one of the brilliant Meccan nobles, led his squadron to the unprotected rear of the Muslim formation. Catching them unawares, he began a great slaughter. The Prophet's uncle Hamzah was felled by a skilled Meccan javelin thrower, and Muhammad himself, though protected by twenty of his closest followers, was knocked off his horse. One of his teeth was broken, his face gashed, a lip bruised. Abu Sufyan had even dared to hope that Muhammad might die from his wounds. When he began to taunt the defeated Muslim troops, Muhammad sent his trusted lieutenant, 'Umar, to give him the riposte: "God is most high and most glorious," shouted 'Umar. "We are not equal: our dead are in paradise, yours in hell, and by God, you have not killed the Prophet. He is listening to us even as we speak!"[19]

Not only was Muhammad listening, but he also had resolved to learn the deeper lesson behind this bitter defeat. The defeat of Uhud became as important for Islam as the victory of Badr. The fate of Muslims always rests with God:

He knows what lies between their hands and behind them.
Q 2.255 (Ayat al-Kursi: the Throne verse)

In defeat as in victory the Muslims had to acknowledge that their fate is not theirs but God's to decide.

The aftermath of the Battle of Uhud also reinforced Muhammad's resolve to secure the loyalty of all his followers—both those who were Muslims and those who were non-Muslims yet bound to him by treaty. There followed some difficult, often bloody purges of tribes near Medina, then a major battle in 627—the Battle of the Trench. A mighty Meccan army was led again by Abu Sufyan, the architect of Uhud. Abu Sufyan had hoped to invade Medina, to defeat and destroy Muslims once and for all. Yet again, God had granted Muslims victory there, and God had granted them more than a military victory; fierce foes like Abu Sufyan and also the fiery Khalid ibn al-Walid had seen the truth of the Qur'an. They had embraced Islam and become Muslims.

Final Years

After the Battle of the Trench, Muhammad never ceased trying to win the Meccans over to the religion of Islam. He undertook a peaceful pilgrimage. He contacted the Meccans and assured their leaders of his intention. Still, they doubted him. It took until 629, seven years after he had left Mecca, before he and his followers were allowed to reenter their native city. At last all Muslims—those

Meccans who had immigrated to Medina, those Medinans who had joined them, and other tribes who had become their allies, then also submitted to God—all were able to return to Mecca in a peaceful pilgrimage.

The year was 630. The month was January. The sight of the returning Meccans melted the hearts of many who had been their bitter enemies, even though others feared that Muhammad would take vengeance on them. Muhammad forgave all but his bitterest enemies. In his compassion he mirrored the Source of Compassion, and the Almighty granted Muslims Mecca as their reclaimed home, it became the center of their life and faith as Muslims.

As the tenth year of the *hijra* drew to a close, Muhammad experienced the fullness of time. It was the end of Safar, the beginning of First Rabi'a in 632 CE, or 10 AH in the new, lunar calendar that had begun in 622 with Muhammad's flight from his native town. He had just finished praying for the dead at the local cemetery when the pains began. They were fierce, intense, abdominal pains. They never stopped. They took his life, fulfilling yet another of God's promises:

Every soul must know the taste of death.
Then you will be sent back to Us.
    Q 29:57[20]

The life story of Muhammad was only the beginning of Islam. Muslim armies expanded across much of the civilized world surrounding the Mediterranean and Indian Oceans, and with their expansion the Arabic Qur'an was not only used but also translated into Muslim languages. It is the story of that expanded process of translation, beyond Muslim languages into European languages, that provides the crucial antecedent to the *Koran* in English.

The Orientalist *Koran*

CHAPTER 2

Early Attempts at Translation into Latin

In *After Babel*, George Steiner proposes the central question of translation: "Should a good translation edge its own language towards that of the original, thus creating a deliberate aura of strangeness, of peripheral opaqueness? Those who privilege the original text would answer in the affirmative. Or should a good translation naturalize the character of the linguistic import so as to make it at home in the speech of the translator and readers? Those who privilege the target audience, would answer 'yes.'"[1]

This rehearsal of the problem of translation is not foreign or peripheral to the subject of translating the Qur'an. It had recurred in the early centuries of Islamic history, and among its earliest practitioners were European Christians at the time of the Crusades, intent on understanding the Muslim enemy. Polemics—opposing the enemy—was also intermingled with philology—understanding the enemy, and both approaches were embraced by those later known as Orientalists, that is, those who study the East or the Orient, in this case, the Muslim East, which is also the Muslim West, since the Muslim world by the eighth century had already spanned North Africa as well as South Asia.[2]

What recent scholarship has demonstrated is just how effective were some of the earliest non-Muslim translators in communicating the truth of the Qur'an/*Koran* in Latin, itself the stepping-stone to later efforts of translation into modern European languages, including English. The foremost was also the earliest Latin translator: Robert of Ketton (d. 1160). Robert established a high bar of philological accuracy, not distorting but disclosing the meaning of the Arabic in Latin, a practice that others followed in English translations. In short, however much some non-Muslims may have disagreed with the particular prophecy reshaped in Arabic and announced through Muhammad, they still wanted to understand in clear Latin the same message that had been earlier communicated in seventh-century Arabic.

Translation is hard work, never more so than when translating a scripture from its original language into another. To ponder the meaning of esoteric words is to explore the signs of other realities and then render them into their lyrical equivalents. Translators must know that other language—its grammar, its rhetoric, and its ambivalences—as well as they know their own. That is the challenge faced by all foragers of the foreign, those who enter into others' mental space with the intent of linking it to their own.

To move from Latin to Arabic is to move from a language with all its antecedents in citied life, where roads and properties, irrigation and water tanks, armies and taxes matter most, to a desert life, where tribes are the norm, spaces open, oases the lifeline for survival, and cities but dots etched on emptiness. It is not just that Latin and Arabic are different alphabets and grammars; they also reflect histories and societies even more disparate than their speech and writing.

How then can one hope to translate from Qur'anic Arabic, the quintessential language of the desert, into High Latin, the expressive language of medieval cosmopolitan culture? This form of translation is not just hard work; it is the hardest work.

For an educated twelfth-century Englishman, proficiency in Latin was natural. Robert of Ketton studied Latin because it was the language of both theology and science. But Latin was more advanced in theology, thanks to Augustine and Jerome, than it was in science. The rudiments of mathematics and astronomy were just becoming known in twelfth-century Europe. They were becoming better and better known thanks to translations from Arabic into Latin coming out of southern Spain or Andalusia. Cities like Seville and Cordoba remained both Muslim and Arab while cities that had been recaptured by Castilian Christians, like Badajoz and Toledo, retained links to their Andalusian past. Since the tenth century, scholars of philosophy and the sciences had been working with translations from Greek to Syriac, then to Arabic, and now to Latin. It was to Barcelona that Robert first went, in 1136. There he studied Arabic with Plato of Tivoli before finding the employment that he had sought, the one that gave him the most satisfaction, and much-needed remuneration: translating scientific works in astronomy and geometry but especially algebra. He belonged to a school of translators known from their location in that medieval center of cosmopolitan life, Toledo.

Toledan translators were part of a Catholic Christian society that was not neutral about religion. Hand in hand with converting ancient Greek wisdom into medieval European science was the desire to convert Muslims into Christians. In 1142 when the Abbot of Cluny, Peter the Venerable, visited Toledo, he asked Robert of Ketton to lead a team project. The goal was to produce the first Latin version of the Holy Qur'an. Well, not exactly "Holy" since in the eyes of both Robert and his patron Peter, Muhammad was a charlatan rather than a true prophet, and the book he produced less than a divine decree. Robert had once before tried his hand at religious Arabic. He had produced an anthology of essays about Muhammad in Latin. It was titled *Saracen Fables or Lies and Ridiculous Tales from the Saracens*. This new undertaking—to translate the Qur'an—also expressed contempt for its human subject. Its title was *The Law of the Pseudo-Prophet Muhammad and the Arabic* Koran.[3] It was completed between 1141 and 1143.

Consider the time of this undertaking. It was the mid-twelfth century. The First Crusade had just been fought; in 1099 Jerusalem had been seized on behalf of the pope. But Turkish/Muslim forces regrouped, and not long after Robert's translation was completed, the Turks took Edessa, in 1144. There then followed the Second Crusade

(1147–49), and the Third Crusade (1189–92). All had papal approval. All marshaled Christian support against a Muslim adversary. Throughout the twelfth and into the thirteenth centuries, European Christendom had a double mission: to slay Muslims and to retake Christian lands occupied by infidel Moors.

In such a charged atmosphere, the effort to "honor" the pseudo-prophet of Islam by translating his lies (the Qur'an) was itself an ecumenical act. Peter the Venerable was more than Robert's patron. He also spurred the Christian initiative to understand, rather than vilify, Islam. While Peter wanted to expose the falsehood of the Qur'an, he also believed that one had to have information about its content before confronting—and hopefully defeating—Muslim adversaries. Peter was advocating battle of the word rather than battle by the sword, even at a time when the crusader mentality was on the ascendant. It may seem that most European Christians, including the pope, had already made up their mind about the evil of Islam and the falsehood of the Qur'an. Peter suggests as much when he calls (in vain) for Islam to be approached, not "as our people often do, by arms, but by words; not by force, but by reason; not in hatred, but in love."[4]

Legacy of Robert of Ketton

Robert's effort at translation had consequences. His translation did find an audience. It was copied into numerous manuscripts, and then when the printing press became available in the sixteenth century, not only was the Gutenberg Bible published but also two Latin editions of Robert of Ketton's translation of the Qur'an. As one scholar has observed, "When European Christians read the Qur'an any time between the mid-twelfth and late seventeenth century, they usually read Robert's version."[5] There is little doubt, for instance, that Martin Luther, when he wanted to assess the scriptural outlook of his Turkish Muslim enemies, read the translation done by Robert of Ketton four hundred years earlier.[6]

Blind hatred may not have been replaced by enlightened engagement but at least a version of the Qur'an became available in a European language, and some were trying to make sense of its signs.

And for Robert of Ketton, translating the Qur'an posed a special challenge. It was a challenge of a different order than translating scientific texts from Arabic into Latin. One could not rely on a literal rendition of Arabic, as was the case for the sophisticated urban Arabic of scientific texts. Scientific Arabic was not the same as Qur'anic Arabic. The former was language that had been developed after the time of the Prophet Muhammad and the first generation of Muslims. But Qur'anic Arabic projected a desert culture, one that preceded Robert by more than five centuries, one that was remote from him and his European contemporaries.

Robert could have produced a literal translation, and later scholars have faulted him for what seemed to be his loose, almost subjective rendition of the Qur'an, but that was not the case. Robert believed enough in the revelatory claims of the Qur'an to consult Muslims who had written commentaries. He consulted many such commentaries, including Tabari's famed *tafsīr*, and while he never cited them by name, it is very clear that he used them, and preferred them to a literal rendering, especially of difficult passages.

Simply because "The Law of the Pseudo-Prophet Muhammad and the Arabic *Koran*" is a paraphrase does not mean that it is a poor and misleading translation, especially since Robert was trying to gauge what Muslims themselves took the Qur'an to mean. Robert understood what many of his European successors who attempted to translate the Qur'an did not: there was a long tradition of Arabic/Muslim commentary, and it could be beneficial to moving between different languages, cultures, and religions. Robert used Muslim Qur'an commentaries, whether through translation or by reference to them in Arabic, and he based his own "loose" translations of difficult words or complex passages on readings gleaned from these same commentaries.

Time and again, Robert projects himself as peacefully disposed to the same enemy whom many of his co-religionists were intent on killing. Could it perhaps be that his outward antipathy for the Qur'an was a ruse against his enemies, a pose to deflect their animosity? In the atmosphere of the Crusades, and engaged by a patron (Peter the Venerable) already suspect for his irenic views, Robert had to be harsh on Muhammad; he had to denounce "his book of lies." Yet Robert's careful labor, his use of Muslim commentaries to understand what

Muslims themselves believed to be the Qur'anic message, marked him as one with inward sympathy for Islam and also for the Book or "Law of Muhammad." He was an Orientalist with a lyrical ear and a light heart.

The paradox of admiring your enemy is one not easily grasped by those who have never translated. You may dislike someone or some idea, but still try to understand both the person and the concept that are alien to you. If Islam is what you dislike, and the Qur'an is the heart of Islam, then you have to resort to Muslims who believe in Muhammad's message in order to grasp what they "mistakenly" think to be its truth. Although hostile to Islam, Robert was willing to trust Muslim scholars in trying to unravel what Muslims found believable in the "false" prophecy of Muhammad. This was, after all, no ordinary book. It was a holy book, or so it claimed.

Earliest English Translation: Ross

We can review the final product, but we cannot probe the deep reflex, of Robert or his successors. From the twelfth century on, several non-Muslim scholars rendered into Latin the Arabic Qur'an, at once the lodestone of truth and the object of rivalry for these Christian translators. Their mixed motivations are sometimes signaled in prefaces. They give at least some of the reasons motivating a particular translation at a certain time and place, and they allow a provisional construction of the role of the translator in each specific instance, but what is sorely lacking is the motives of each translator for specific choices at each juncture, with each decision, to translate a particular sura. What Burman says of Robert can be repeated for others: "We will never know how Robert himself would have explained or justified the choices he made as a translator."[7]

What is known is the motive for some of those translators who took up the task in English from the seventeenth century on. The first complete *English* translation of the Qur'an to be published was that of Alexander Ross, a chaplain to King Charles I, in 1649. It is actually translated from a French translation by André du Ryer published in 1647. In other words, Ross did not know Arabic, as had Robert and earlier Arabic-to-Latin translators. Instead he relies on the labor and erudition of Du Ryer. Du Ryer had had an extensive and illustrious diplomatic career in Nile-to-Oxus posts that allowed him to learn Turkish, Arabic, and possibly also Persian. His translation of the Qur'an was actually the oldest to ever be done into a European vernacular, and like Robert, he made repeated and constructive use of Islamic commentaries. He also made dismissive comments about Muhammad as a prophet in his preface, again following Robert's example, but one may conjecture that he too shared more sympathy with the text than his biting preface suggested.[8]

Between 1649 and 1856, Ross's translation of Du Ryer went through some eight editions both in Britain and the United States. It was titled *The Alcoran of Mahomet, translated out of Arabick into French by the Sieur du Ryer, and newly Englished, for the satisfaction of all that desire to look into the Turkish vanities.* The tone is combative. The derogatory reference to the Turks reflects that the Ottoman Empire, although checked by Hapsburgs and Russians, still loomed large as a threat in the contemporary European consciousness of the time. (The Ottomans would besiege Vienna one last time in 1683.) The attribution of the Qur'an to "Mahomet," of course, follows a pattern of attributing the Book to Muhammad as its author, rather than Allah/God as the divine source. That diminution of its scriptural authority goes back to Robert of Ketton and is repeated throughout the history of Western scholarship. But Ross reflects a kind of Protestant missionary reflex when he adds to his long title not only a confirmation of Mahomet as the author but also "a needful Caveat or Admonition for them who desire to know what use may be made of, or if there be any danger in, reading the Alcoran."

Landmark *Koran* Translation: Sale

After the translation of Ross, almost a century passed before a new *Koran* translation in English was published, and that new translation became a landmark in the history of the *Koran*. It was the 1734 translation by George Sale. For over 200 years, his translation persisted as the longest lasting, most popular, and influential English translation, having gone through at least 123 editions in both Britain and the United States up to 1975. For most

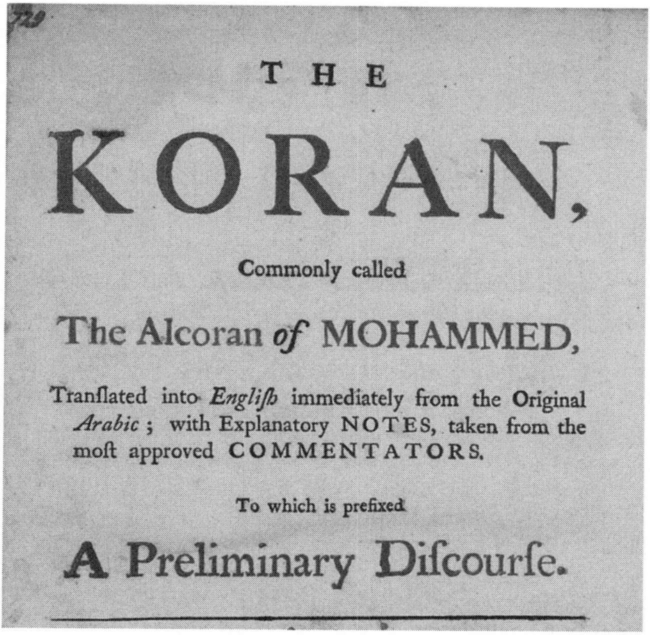
THE

KORAN,

Commonly called

The Alcoran *of* MOHAMMED,

Tranſlated into *Engliſh* immediately from the Original *Arabic*; with Explanatory NOTES, taken from the moſt approved COMMENTATORS.

To which is prefixed

A Preliminary Diſcourſe.

FIGURE 1. Cover for the first edition of George Sale's translation of *The Koran*. Courtesy of the Rubenstein Library at Duke University

English readers it was *the* Qur'an of record. It was certainly the Qur'an that Thomas Jefferson not only bought in 1765 but also consulted frequently in the early years of the Republic.[9]

Sale is both like and unlike Ross in his motivation. Although a lawyer by profession and not a Christian cleric like Ross, Sale had previously filled an appointment as one of the correctors of the Arabic New Testament published by the Society for the Promotion of Christian

Knowledge (SPCK), and it is through SPCK connections, specifically with two Syrian Christians living in England, Salmon Negri and Carolus Dadichi, that "Sale learned, or at least perfected, his Arabic."[10] Unlike Ross, however, Sale did not rely on the translator of another European vernacular but instead the Latin translation of Marracci (1698), about which he says: "Though it adheres to the Arabic idiom too literally to be easily understood, I should be guilty of ingratitude, did I not acknowledge myself much obliged thereto; but still being in Latin it can be of no use to those who understand not that tongue."[11]

Yet like Ross, Sale seems to justify his labor as a necessary, and he hopes effective, attack on the "Mohammedans." In his "Preliminary Discourse," he argues that "the Protestants alone are able to attack the *Koran* with success; and for them, I trust, Providence has reserved the glory of its overthrow," and he returns repeatedly to the human nature of the book's origin: Muhammad merely "pretended" to receive his revelations and claimed a divine origin for them in order to facilitate his effort to unite the Arab tribes and to enhance his prestige and power.

So salacious was Sale's "Preliminary Discourse" that it appeared not only with later editions of Sale's translation, it was also independently printed and translated into a number of languages. "A Sketch of the Life of George Sale" was added to editions of Sale's translation in 1825, despite the fact that the preface declares that Sale, in his elegant and winsome translation,[12] was actually equating

Islam with Christianity, and was perhaps secretly himself a "Mohammedan"!

The subtlety and ambiguity of Sale's labor requires close reading of his *Koran* translation. Of the many instances where Sale's expansive rendition could be mistaken as closet conversion to Islam, one certainly would be the final chapter, Q 114, which he titles "The Chapter of Men":

> *In the Name of the Most Merciful God.*
>
> *Say, I fly for refuge unto the Lord of men, the king of men, the God of men, that he may deliver me from the mischief of the whisperer who slyly withdraweth, who whispereth evil suggestions into the breasts of men; from genii and men.*

In tone, if not in wording, this follows the example of Robert of Ketton. The key hope is expressed by Robert as "defend and free thee," while for Sale, who highlights the crucial phrase, the same invocation is rendered "that he may deliver me." Although he does not mention "the Devil" in the text, as does Robert, Sale includes it in a footnote indicating that "the whisperer who slyly with-draweth" is "the Devil; who withdraweth when a man mentioneth God, or hath recourse to his protection."

But even more pronounced is Sale's rendition, then his footnote, to Q 2:62, oft cited by Abrahamic pluralists as confirmation of the expansive notion of salvation announced in the Qur'an:

> *Surely those who believe, and those who Judaise, and Christians,*

> *And Sabians,* [Sale footnote] *whoever believeth in GOD,*
> *and the last day, and doth that which is right, they*
> *shall have their reward with their LORD; there shall*
> *come no fear on them, neither shall they be grieved.*

It is the footnote that signals Sale's sympathies with a soteriology that is inclusive. After reviewing the naysayers, he declares that other commentators interpret this passage to mean: "'That no man, whether he be a *Jew*, a *Christian*, or a *Sabian*, shall be excluded from salvation, provided he quit his erroneous religion and become a *Moslem*.' Interestingly, a parallel statement is found in the New Testament: 'In every nation he that feareth GOD, and worketh righteousness, is accepted with him' (Acts 10:35), from which it must be inferred that the religion of nature, or any other, is sufficient to save, without faith in Christ."[13]

While others have looked at this passage with hope for all "true" believers, it is a signal mark of Sale's openness to Islam, and the Qur'anic message, that he could declare in his commentary on Q 2:62: "it must be inferred that the religion of nature, *or any other*, is sufficient to save, without faith in Christ." It is as if Sale is echoing the same reflex noted by Ibn Khaldun, to wit, one must account for the motive of the Divine author of *all* life, the One who created both Magians and muslims. Even those who adhere to "the religion of nature, or any other" might be saved in the infinite expanse of Divine mercy. Certainly, no Protestant evangelist or

Christian triumphalist or "orthodox" Muslim could accept such an interpretation of Divine writ, whether in Acts of the Apostles or in the Arabic Qur'an. Jefferson must have found in Sale's commentary an echo of his own liberal disposition on matters of creedal assertion and cosmic hope.

Sale and Robert of Ketton

Even as one probes and praises Sale, it is important to note, as Alexander Bevilacqua has pointed out, that "Sale's translation employs some of the paratactic structures as well as the falling metre of the King James Bible. Similarity in content (King James Version, Luke 1:34: 'Then said Mary unto the angel, How shall this be, seeing I know not a man?') is thus amplified by similarity in style. It helps that a feature of Hebrew poetry which the King James Bible made familiar to Anglophone audiences, the use of parallelism and repetition, is also a major stylistic feature of the Qur'an (here, 'seeing a man hath not touched me, and I am no harlot')."[14]

Yet the closest antecedent to Sale is not the KJV of the Bible but the translation style of Robert of Ketton in his Latin rendition of the Qur'an. "Perhaps Sale's version has enjoyed more recognition than Marracci's," observes Bevilacqua, "not only on account of the latter's polemic but also because Sale's *Koran* conforms more recognisably to what a proper translation could be: *a text with the ambition, ideally, of replacing its source* (as unattainable as this may be in the case of the Qur'an). Marracci's more literal effort, with its accompanying Arabic original, does not seek to replace its source text. As such, it occupies a less prestigious status, somewhere between an interlinear paraphrase and a freestanding translation. Yet *Sale's choices as translator signaled a return, mutatis mutandis, to the elevated stylistics of Robert of Ketton's medieval version*, as opposed to the Renaissance philological tradition which culminated in Marracci's work."[15]

The Turn toward Muhammad: Rodwell

Beyond Sale, there were two other nineteenth-century British/English translations that merit sustained attention. Rev. J. M. Rodwell first published his effort in 1861. Although less popular than Sale's, which saw over 170 editions in every corner of the English-speaking world, Rodwell's *The Koran* was well received, and it became especially widespread when it was reissued as part of the series "Everyman's Library" beginning in 1909. It subsequently went through some fifty editions in both Britain and the United States by 2002.

Rodwell no longer talks about "overthrowing the Mohammedan heresy," as had Sale and others of previous generations. Instead, there is a focus on the person of Muhammad. In the introduction to his translation, Rodwell declares: "To speak of the *Koran* is ... practically the same as speaking of Muhammad," since there is a "complete identity between the literary work and the mind of the man who produced it."[16] The motivation for translation is therefore to gain insight into Muhammad's mind, and while one could object that this approach misunderstands the thrust of Muslim theology, it is still less carping or proselytizing than his predecessors.

But Rodwell goes one step further: he completely rearranges the *sūra*s, or chapters of the Qur'an. He places them into chronological order so that the reader can "trace the development of the prophet's mind." He signals his intent in the very title of his translation: *The Koran; Translated from the Arabic, the Suras arranged in chronological order with notes*. Fortunately, the translation is provided with a table that coordinates Rodwell's rearrangement with the traditional order of the *sūra*s. According to Rodwell, the reader will find: (1) that Muhammad perverted prior Christian and Jewish traditions to suit his own purpose (reflecting the recurrent Western charge that Muhammad was merely a syncretistic plagiarizer and that Islam is thus totally derived from its Jewish and Christian antecedents); and (2) that Muhammad was a manic-depressive epileptic, liable to hallucinations, who "worked himself up into a belief that he had received a divine call."[17] The motivation for translating the Qur'an, one could argue, is still to undermine Islam, but this strategy has taken on the form less of an attack on the text of the Qur'an itself than on the person of the prophet, whom the text of the Qur'an presumably embodies and from whom it originates. Despite the flaws and shortcomings in Rodwell's theology, his text still has a resonance that appeals to those who engage the *Koran* as outsiders.[18]

A Proto-Scientific Approach: Palmer

The year 1880 heralded a fresh academic attempt to translate and understand the *Koran* in English. Edward Henry Palmer, a Cambridge scholar and translator of Arabic, Persian, Urdu, and Turkish, published his work as *The Qur'an, Translated*. Separating itself from the popularizing Anglicized name of its predecessors, *The Qur'an, Translated* appeared as part of the series "Sacred Books of the East" (volumes 6 and 9), both published by Oxford University Press, which later republished the set as part of its sequel series "The World's Classics." Palmer's translation went through several editions in Britain, perhaps as many as thirty, and was reprinted in the United States as late as 1965.

In the historical introduction to his translation, Palmer, like Rodwell, views Muhammad as a hallucinating, deceiving epileptic, but unlike Rodwell he does not rearrange the order of the *sūra*s of the Qur'an. He writes as one who believes that the message itself can be understood in clear, plain English. "My endeavor," he writes in the preface, "[is] to set before the reader plainly what the Qur'an is and what it contains." In other words, he eschews the earlier Christian polemic against Islam explicit in previous translations and offers in its place a seemingly scientific and detached desire to present the text as it is.

Critics have questioned, however, whether or not his colloquial English did, in fact, capture what he himself termed the "rude and rugged" Arabic of the original.[19]

The Twentieth-Century Explosion: Asian Muslim Translations

While the legacy of the nineteenth century offered new avenues to the *Koran* in English, it still did not anticipate what occurred in the following century. The twentieth century augured directions that cut across the models, the approaches, and the outcomes of the efforts from Sale to Palmer. It saw *Koran* translations by Muslims appear at a dizzying pace as the century wound through two world wars, independence movements, colonial and postcolonial jolts. It did finally seem that English could become, as one translator asserted, "an Islamic language." There was not only heightened attention to renditions of the *Koran* into English but also to imitation of earlier models across confessional lines—Muslim/non-Muslim—but also across sectarian lines—Shiʿi, Sunni, and Ahmadi.

For nearly eight centuries, beginning with Robert of Ketton in the early twelfth centuryh and culminating in the late nineteenth century with E. H. Palmer, one could sense a debate not about the issue of translation itself but about how best to translate. All their efforts might be framed as respectful borrowing (in the case of Robert) or parasitic imitation (in the case of Ross). Yet *both* judgments pertain to most translations. In some cases, there is acknowledgment of previous efforts, as Sale does with Marracci, or even earlier Ross with Du Ryer.

Yet the term *parasitic* has a general sense that applies in all cases. In its original meaning, *parasitic* applies to plants that climb on and feed off another plant in order to grow, or to those who eat at another's table without reciprocating. Both the natural and the commensal models apply. Not all translators were competent linguists, some were parasites in the narrower, nastier sense of that term, but almost all translators were parasitical in the larger sense, drawing on the best of what they had inherited, or to which they had access, from antecedent scholars who had been motivated by the same quest and perplexed by the same text. On this spectrum of comparison—between clear originality and rank plagiarism—Muslims as well as non-Muslims can be and should be ranked. It is not a matter of creedal loyalty but of honesty, diligence, even doggedness. From the mid-nineteenth century on, Western scholars and Christian missionaries were encountering efforts to revitalize Islam in the face of westernization. The printing press, along with rail and ship communications, facilitated Muslim efforts to reclaim not just the Arabic Qur'an but also the English *Koran* as their Book, and so to project Islam as the final, pure, and triumphant religion.

Overshadowing the Muslim efforts, however, there is a clamor for orthodoxy not present in the non-Muslim translations just reviewed. One finds within Muslim debates a particular manifestation of the ambiguity or tension expressed by the phrase *traduttore traditore*. On the one hand, many assert that *any* translation of the Qur'an into another language amounts to a betrayal of the Word of God and of the ideal of unity among all Muslims, under one faith and one language. Translations are seen as the work of outsiders, such as Christian missionaries, who seek only to undermine Islam. But on the other hand, and at the same time, these non-Muslim translations sparked the desire to produce authentically Muslim translations that would highlight the meaning of the Qur'an while conforming to the demands of orthodoxy. Entering the long twentieth century, the debates within Islam regarding translation of the Arabic Qur'an provide more than a tug of war between Muslim and non-Muslim translators. What we witness instead is the explosion of *Koran* translations by and for Muslims. It takes place in South Asia and among Asian Muslims. It is this South Asian engagement with the *Koran* in English to which I now turn.

The South Asian *Koran*

CHAPTER 3

Preamble

No one could have anticipated what the twentieth century would bring to the world of Islam and to the prospect of translating the *Koran* into English. The midwife for English was not Arabia but Asia. By the late eighteenth century, much of Mughal India had come under the rule of the British East India Company. South Asia became the testing ground for experiments with English that impacted both the colonizer and the colonized. After 1813 Christian missionaries were allowed to proselytize in the subcontinent. Although they enjoyed little success, even Indians with no interest in religion were affected when, in 1832, the official language switched from Persian to English; educational curricula as well as administrative exams became Anglicized. A revolt in 1857 led to the imposition of direct British rule, after which the prestige and prevalence of English in the public domain accelerated still further; most talented Indians regarded proficiency in English as indispensable for advancement in any profession. It is no surprise then that South Asia became the incubator for *Koran* translation projects. The intent of Indian Muslim translators was to use English to succeed, with religion as well as with commerce.

In this chapter I will review four major South Asian translators: initially Muhammad Ali, Muhammad Marmaduke Pickthall, and Yusuf Ali, then much later, Muhammad Asad. In addition to these four major translators, several other South Asian Muslims, whether scholars or laymen, attempted translations that are seldom discussed, or else only mentioned in passing. Yet all of them—both the famous few and the unacknowledged many—were motivated to produce a book, not any book but the Noble Book, the Word of God, in English.[1]

From the dawn of the twentieth century to the outbreak of World War II, in the entire realm of the British Raj, there appeared the following translations of the *Koran* into English: Muhammad Abdul Hakim Khan 1905, Mirza Abul Fazl 1910, Hairat Dihlawi 1916, Maulana Muhammad Ali 1917, Ghulam Sarwar 1920, Marmaduke Pickthall 1930, Yusuf Ali 1934–37. In other words, in less than forty years seven Muslims, including a British convert who lived in India (Pickthall), produced more *Koran* translations than all of the British Orientalists from the preceding three centuries (Ross—seventeenth, Sale—eighteenth, Palmer and Rodwell—nineteenth).[2]

Ahmadi Forerunner: Muhammad Ali

Even more astonishing than the rate of production is the sequence of its producers. The pioneer of major *Koran* translators from the Indian subcontinent was Muhammad

Ali. Although I had long admired his work, I only became aware of Ali's pervasive impact as *Koran* translator when I visited Aligarh Muslim University in 2014. I was invited to have tea with an English professor, who is also an avid reviewer of *Koran* translations. Over an extended conversation, Abdur Raheem Kidwai presented me a book about his ancestor, Maulana Abdul Majid Daryabadi (d. 1977). Daryabadi, a highly regarded Sunni Muslim scholar, belongs to that large cohort of noted scholars from the Asian subcontinent who pursued their own, lesser translations of the *Koran*. Most appeared in print only after World War II.

Maulana Abdul Majid Daryabadi had already finished his magnum opus in the early 1930s. Although it had been partially published during World War II, he could not secure a publisher of the full version until after the formation of Pakistan (1947). Finally published in 1957, it was titled *The Holy Qur'an: Translated from the original Arabic, with lexical, grammatical, historical, geographical, and eschatological comments, and explanations and sidelights on comparative religion*. It is highlighted in Kidwai's biography of Daryabadi, *From Darkness into Light* (2013). Daryabadi, after straying from Islam in his youth, had been brought back to the fold by no less a figure than Maulana Muhammad Ali. There is much praise for Muhammad Ali, especially for his dedication to journalism as a means to promote interest in and attachment to Islam. "Muhammad Ali's genius reflected amply in his impeccable English, his rhetorical speeches across the country, his towering public figure and his journalistic accomplishments overwhelmed Daryabadi."[3] Indeed, "through his profound remarks, Muhammad Ali instilled religious fervor into the young Daryabadi, turning him into a deeply committed and unswerving champion of Islam."[4] Despite these high plaudits for Muhammad Ali, echoing those provided by Haji Hafiz Ghulam Sarwar in 1920, Kidwai goes on to say that Muhammad Ali's *Koran* translation (1917), along with an earlier translation by Muhammad Abdul Hakim Khan (1905), "were by Qadyanis [that is, those who followed the teachings and revered the insight of Ghulam Ahmad Qadyani] and hence were patently unreliable."[5]

Underlying the contradictions in Kidwai's narrative is not just demotion of Ahmadi interest in *Koran* translation but also the larger diachronic canvas, what I have termed the anvil of history. From their formation in the late nineteenth century, the Ahmadis had been crucial producers and promoters of *Koran* translation, in India and beyond. They were at the forefront of British colonial subjects who responded to the impact of Protestant missions to India. A product of British rule, they spoke back to their rulers, becoming global proselytizers for Islam. The notion that the Truth resided in a Book had always been central to consideration of the Qur'an, but before the twentieth century it had not been applied to the Qur'an in translation. Translations were made into several European languages, French, German, and English, but gradually English had come to center stage because of the continued use of English during British colonial rule in Africa (Nigeria, Sudan, Egypt) but even more in Asia (the Indian subcontinent, that is, present-day Afghanistan, Pakistan, India, Sri Lanka, and Bangladesh) as well as

Singapore, Malaysia, and the English-speaking population of Indonesia. While the use of English pervaded commercial and clerical classes in early nineteenth-century India, it only extended to the general public during the period of direct British rule in the subcontinent (1857–1947) and continued beyond that time, during the independence era.

Maulana Muhammad Ali was a product of the late nineteenth-century missionary fervor that spurred the Ahmadiyya movement. It attracted upper-class Punjabi Muslims who coalesced around Mirza Ghulam Ahmad (d. 1908), a charismatic figure and prolific writer who made controversial claims to being the Messiah, the Mahdi, and also the *mujaddid* (or Renewer) of Islam. While Mirza Ghulam and his followers engaged in debate with Christian missionaries, they also embraced Christian proselytizing strategies. If Christians proselytized in the East, Ahmadis returned the favor; they mounted sustained missionary efforts in the West. They sent emissaries but also books to both the United Kingdom and the United States, especially major urban centers. Mirza Ghulam had proposed a "*jihad* by the pen," and among his followers that meant the publication of pamphlets, books, journals, and also translations of the Qur'an.

Based in the Lahore branch of this rapidly growing Muslim sect,[6] Muhammad Ali boasted exceptional credentials. A graduate of Government College Lahore, with an MA in English and an LLB in law, he also taught mathematics before joining the Ahmadi movement. He hoped to put forth a new vision of Islam. He embraced the challenge of making the Arabic original accessible through fresh, engaging English. He began his project in 1909 and eight years later published *The Holy Qur'an: With English Translation and Commentary*. Muhammad Ali continuously revised the initial 1917 edition, and from the fourth revision in 1951 until the present, every edition has been copyrighted by Ahmadiyya Anjuman Isha'at Islam. Although its organizational base remains in Lahore, the actual publisher varies according to the language, and the English language version of Muhammad Ali, reflecting Ahmadi missionary work in the United States, is now published in Columbus, Ohio.

Ghulam Sarwar's 1920 rendition further underscores the impact of Maulana Muhammad Ali. Unlike Mirza Abul Fazl and Hairat Dihlawi, who were zealous laymen innocent of scholarly background, Ghulam Sarwar was a trained judge and also a civil servant; he was posted to Singapore from 1896 to 1928. He had both the means and the skills to undertake a *Koran* translation. He acknowledges his indebtedness to Orientalist predecessors—Sale, Rodwell, and Palmer—but, above all, to Muhammad Ali. In effect, Ghulam Sarwar serves as a bridge between Orientalist and South Asian efforts to translate the *Koran*. About Muhammad Ali, he observes: "There is no other translation or commentary of the Holy Qur'an in the English language to compete with Maulvi Muhammad Ali's masterpiece. For ten years past I have always carried Maulvi Muhammad Ali's translation wherever I have been to. It has traveled with me around the globe, has been to Mecca on pilgrimage, to the London Conference of Religions of 1924, and to all places and assemblies of men that I have been to."[7] Even when he objects to the English style of Muhammad Ali's translation, he does so lightly, almost mocking himself as much as his predecessor. "The translation of the Qur'an," he concludes, "is somewhat like playing a game of chess. Everyone may learn to play the game, but no one has yet exhausted the knowledge thereof.

Wa fawqa kulli dhī 'ilmin 'alīm

And above everyone having knowledge
there is one having more."[8]
    Q 12:76

Yet in the 1920s, at the same time that Ghulam Sarwar was traveling with Muhammad Ali's translation in his pocket, there were debates about Ahmadi loyalty to Muhammad as the Final Prophet. Skeptical Egyptian authorities refused to authorize *The Holy Qur'an*.[9] Others have followed suit, and today the naysayers include many webmasters whose taxonomies of *Koran* translations demote or deride Muhammad Ali (see chapter 4, "The Virtual *Koran* and Beyond").

Orthodox opposition, however, seems to have increased rather than reduced the appeal of Muhammad Ali's carefully crafted rendition. Vigorous efforts to promote the book gave it international notoriety that continues until today. In North America, *The Holy Qur'an* became especially influential among African American Muslim communities, to such an extent that the paper *Muhammad Speaks* printed portions of the translation frequently, though without acknowledging the author.

Elijah Muhammad, leader of the Nation of Islam, was among those who relied on *The Holy Qur'an*. He quoted it directly in several books. He even encouraged his readers to study specific footnotes contained in Muhammad Ali's rendition.

The Holy Qur'an also played an important role in England. There it was used in teaching and preaching at the Woking Mission of the Ahmadiyya. Although its twenty-five editions are modest in comparison to the more than 150 for Pickthall, and another 200 for Yusuf Ali, *The Holy Qur'an* has been translated into most European languages. The pioneering effort of the Lahori Ahmadis to publish and distribute English translations on a global scale has placed Muhammad Ali's rendition in the hands of Muslims from Jakarta, Istanbul, and Cairo, from London to Los Angeles.[10] Its historical value exceeds its sectarian origins. While there has been controversy in many places—in India it received a mixed reception, praised by some, pilloried by others, as in Kidwai's assessment above—beyond dispute is the catalytic role that Muhammad Ali enjoyed in the surge to have South Asian Muslims provide for themselves, and for the entire Muslim community, an English *Koran* worthy of the Arabic original.

Itinerant Convert: Muhammad Marmaduke Pickthall

It is unimaginable that Pickthall was not inspired by Muhammad Ali in undertaking his own rendition. But his was a circuitous route. Born toward the end of the nineteenth century, Marmaduke Pickthall made a name for himself first as a novelist and later as a journalist and translator. Attracted to Islam while in India, Pickthall returned to the United Kingdom during World War I. He frequented the Woking Mosque, an Ahmadi mission center linked to Muhammad Ali, as noted above. When, in 1917, Pickthall publicly declared his conversion to Islam, he became one of the highest-profile English converts in history. From 1919, he took over responsibilities for leading prayers and delivering sermons at the mosque. In this capacity, he sometimes used Muhammad Ali's translation in preparing sermons, yet he complained that this effort "seemed nonsense to the English people who came to my services." Translations by Europeans were no better; they treated the Qur'an as "just a book" and turned its majestic Arabic into slack English. Believing that the Qur'an was not just a book for Muslims but a universal message for all humankind, Pickthall began to compose his own renderings for use in the Woking Mosque. When his congregation received them with enthusiasm, he resolved to do his own translation, though not in England.

Returning to India in the early 1920s, he found employment with the Nizam of Hyderabad, one of the world's wealthiest men. In 1928 the Nizam granted Pickthall two years of paid leave in order to complete his translation of the Qur'an. Not content to rely upon his own knowledge, Pickthall consulted both European academics and traditional Islamic scholars during this period. At once a professional writer, a Muslim, and a native speaker of English, Pickthall saw himself as uniquely suited to compose an English translation that would surpass all previous attempts.

Pickthall wanted to consult the ulema of Egypt and to revise his manuscript under their guidance in order to avoid mistakes and "unorthodoxy." Egypt's al-Azhar University remained an important center of Islamic learning when Egypt was under indirect British rule, and by going to Cairo in 1929 for guidance and approval, Pickthall acknowledged the authority of al-Azhar in the global Muslim community. Although he knew of the furor over Muhammad Ali's translation, Pickthall presumed that the Egyptian ulema had issued a fatwa against it because it was a heretical Ahmadi work. Upon his arrival in Alexandria, Pickthall came to learn that the ulema were divided over a larger question, the question of whether *any* translation of the Qur'an was lawful. Not only would he have to revise his translation, he would also have to make the case for translation as an orthodox practice. Pickthall was dismayed by the condescending attitude of the Egyptian scholars toward non-Arab Muslims and considered leaving Egypt for Damascus. But he persevered, and indeed triumphed.

Pickthall's King James style translation became one of the most widely circulated translations in any language. *The Meaning of the Holy Koran* (1930) has enjoyed at least 150 editions and influenced numerous subsequent English translations. In 1996 it was revised by Arafat El-Ashi and republished in 1996 by Amana Books. A further revised edition, edited by Jane McAuliffe, has just been published by W. W. Norton in February 2017. It has been, and will remain, widely used across the English-speaking world.

Special attention should be paid to the first word in its title: *The* Meaning *of the Holy Koran*. This is more than a nod to the strictures of orthodoxy. In order to ensure the distinction between the Qur'an and its translations, Islamic religious authorities do not permit translations of the Noble Book to be titled "the Qur'an." This decision became official, when in 1936, Sheikh Mustafa al-Maraghi, rector of al-Azhar University, formally announced in a letter to the prime minister of the time that translations of the Qur'an into any other language cannot be titled the "Qur'an." Sheikh Maraghi's views resulted in a fatwa, or juridical decree, approved in the same year by the Council of Ministers. One of the stipulations attached to this approval was that translations must be called "a translation of an interpretation of the Qur'an" or "an interpretation of the Qur'an in language X."

As a result of this fatwa, al-Azhar University and other Islamic religious institutions do not endorse or grant permission for translations of the Qur'an unless it is explicitly indicated that they are translations of the "meanings" of the Qur'an. They also require that terms such as "explanation," "interpretation," or "paraphrase" should be inserted to indicate that the work is simply an effort to grapple with the inimitable source text, not its equivalent or its replacement. This is why many English translations of the Qur'an have titles such as "Interpretation of the Meanings of the Noble Qur'an in the English Language,"

"The *Koran* Interpreted," or "The Qur'an: New Interpretation." The hedging on *Koran* translation as a full disclosure of the Arabic Qur'an began with Pickthall and has continued well into the twenty-first century.[11]

Tragic Anglophile: Abdullah Yusuf Ali

Like Pickthall, Yusuf Ali did not intend to be a *Koran* translator, but apart from the accident of fame that links them, and the colonial impact of British rule in India that shaped them, their careers were widely divergent, their views of each other carping and even disdainful.

Born in Gujarat in British India to a wealthy merchant family with a Dawoodi Bohra father, Yusuf Ali received a religious education from childhood. He favored the majority Sunni view of Islam. Eventually, he could, and did, recite the entire Qur'an from memory. He spoke Arabic and English with equal fluency. He belonged to a generation of educated Indians who had internalized a sense of British superiority; they embraced the British Empire as the best hope for the progress and modernization of India. To that end, Yusuf Ali dedicated much of his life to working for the British Crown in official and unofficial capacities. Brilliant and highly able, he was one of few Indians to gain admission in the Indian Civil Service (ICS), the professional corps of administrators that directly governed the subcontinent. After resigning from the ICS, Yusuf Ali served Britain during World War I, and then after the war he worked briefly in the employ of the

Nizam of Hyderabad, though not with the same degree of support as his contemporary, Marmaduke Pickthall.

In the late 1920s, Yusuf Ali returned to London, where he oversaw a study group called the Progressive Islam Association. He also commenced his translation of the Qur'an, composing the work while continuing his active public life. The project consumed him. It became a solitary, nocturnal occupation, at once a relief from, and contrast to, his daytime life, a series of meetings, conferences, and lectures. Yusuf Ali often traveled, and wherever he went, he translated—in different climes, on various continents, and often aboard ocean liners.

In the early 1930s, the poet Muhammad Iqbal recruited Yusuf Ali to be the principal of Islamia College in Lahore, then part of British India. It was in Lahore that he began to publish his carefully crafted renditions. They first appeared in installments, between 1934 and 1937. Published as a single edition in 1937, *The Holy Qur'an: Text, Translation, and Commentary* was already in its third edition one year later.[12] Like Muhammad Ali, Yusuf Ali included a running commentary in the form of footnotes. A bloated rendition (with more than 6,000 footnotes), it was at once unconventional and hybrid, reflecting the wide array of influences on Yusuf Ali. It projected who he was—an Anglophile intellectual no less peripatetic in his tastes than in his travels. English literary classics intrude seamlessly into Qur'anic commentary. Instead of Tabari, Zamakhshari, and Razi, Yusuf Ali invokes Shakespeare, Milton, and Tennyson to illuminate Qur'anic passages. His was, above all, an intensely personal engagement with the Noble Book, the Word of God in Arabic. Remote from the communalist politics of his day, Yusuf Ali viewed Islam as an apolitical force, the Qur'an beckoning each individual to be high minded, meditative, ethical. "Read, study and digest the Holy Book," he urges his co-religionists. "Read slowly, and let it sink into your heart and soul."[13]

The intimate, personal character of *The Holy Qur'an: Text, Translation, and Commentary* contributed to its broad appeal, yet those who knew Yusuf Ali did not embrace his magnum opus with the same enthusiasm as the larger English-reading Muslim public. Muhammad Iqbal, the famed poet and supporter of the Muslim League, never offered a word extolling the new translation. Marmaduke Pickthall was openly disdainful. Pickthall derided the commentary, comparing it to the style of the "chorus in Greek tragedies." The translation itself, in his view, was careless and inexact. With biting sarcasm that hints at his own superior credentials as a devout Muslim, Pickthall snipes that Yusuf Ali's work might be of use to Indian Muslims who "know English better than the teaching of their own Qur'an."[14]

Through these sarcastic jabs, the British convert goes well beyond textual criticism of a collegial laborer on *Koran* translation. Perhaps he was attempting to protect his own translation from a new competitor or, alternately, expressing his disapproval for Yusuf Ali's politics. He may actually have believed that a stand-alone English translation was best advanced by one whose native language was English.

Pickthall's sense of rivalry may have been prescient, for it would be difficult to conclude that *The Meaning of the Holy Koran* surpassed *The Holy Qur'an: Text, Translation, and Commentary*, either in the 1930s, when both were first published, or in succeeding decades. Together they impacted millions of *Koran* readers, and while no other translator of the *Koran* into English has enjoyed the pre-eminence of either Pickthall or Yusuf Ali, yet of the two, the latter has had the greater impact. His *Koran* translation has enjoyed more than 200 editions, compared to the 150 editions of Pickthall's. Not just the original version of Yusuf Ali's epochal work but also its multiple adaptations, even those overriding the author's original intent, attest to the enduring appeal of *The Holy Qur'an: Text, Translation, and Commentary*.[15]

Despite rivalries and disagreements, their deaths, like their lives and labors, link Abdullah Yusuf Ali and Muhammad Marmaduke Pickthall. Late in life Yusuf Ali returned to England. He died in London, destitute and friendless. He was buried at the Muslim cemetery at Brookwood, Surrey, near Woking, where Pickthall had served in the mosque and where Pickthall also was buried. In a strange historical twist, both Yusuf Ali's grave and the grave of his contemporary rival, Marmaduke Pickthall, have now become a combined pilgrimage site for devout Muslims.[16]

Beyond their differences, and their convergences, it is also important to recall their common indebtedness of Yusuf Ali and Pickthall to Muhammad Ali. Like Muhammad Ali, they were talking back to the colonizer, the British Raj, in his own language, and with an appeal to Muslim interests as well as sensibilities. They wanted Islam to succeed, and the *Koran* in English to be the basis of its success in India as well as abroad. Although both Pickthall and Yusuf Ali came to translate the *Koran* by different routes, both led from, and also in Pickthall's case back to, Muhammad Ali. All three of these seminal, early twentieth-century *Koran* translators are *Asian* Muslims; even Pickthall is Indian by adoption if not by birth. None of the authors was a traditional Islamic scholar; each of them embraced aspects of Islamic modernism in distinct combinations. The leader of the Lahore Ahmadi movement Muhammad Ali, the English novelist and convert Marmaduke Pickthall, and the Dawūdi Isma'īlī British loyalist Abdullah Yusuf Ali—all composed very different kinds of translations for very different purposes. Yet collectively, they helped individual Muslims engage in personal study of the Qur'an, at the same time that they created an English-language template for the Noble Book that gave precedence to Muslim sensibilities while countering negative portrayals created by non-Muslims. Above all, their combined efforts introduced the Qur'an to a large and rapidly increasing English readership. They helped normalize and legitimize the genre of *Koran* translation, despite the opposition of al-Azhar, as popularity of *Korans* in English soared throughout the twentieth century.

Forensic Rationalist: Muhammad Asad

In addition to the two Alis and Pickthall, there was a fourth South Asian giant in twentieth-century *Koran* translation. His role is pivotal at many levels, not least for contemporary explorers of the Qur'an with a modern, pragmatic, and rational bent.

His Muslim name was Muhammad Asad, but he began his journey as Leopold Weiss. At the remarkably young age of twenty-two, Weiss became a correspondent for the *Frankfurter Zeitung*, one of the most prestigious newspapers of Germany and Europe. As a journalist, he traveled extensively, mingled with ordinary people, held discussions with Muslim intellectuals, and met heads of state in Palestine, Egypt, Transjordan, Syria, Iraq, Iran, and Afghanistan.

During his travels and through his readings, Weiss's interest in Islam increased as he delved into its scripture, history, and world view. In part, curiosity propelled his explorations, but he also felt something darker—in his words, "a spiritual emptiness, a vague, cynical relativism born out of increasing hopelessness"—from which he needed to escape. He remained agnostic, unable to accept that God spoke to and guided humankind by revelation.

Back in Berlin from the Middle East during his midtwenties, Weiss was traveling with his fiancée when he underwent an electrifying spiritual epiphany. It changed his mind and his life. He described it in an emotive passage that he wrote some thirty years later in his autobiography, *The Road to Mecca*:

> One day—it was in September 1926—Elsa [his future wife] and I found ourselves travelling in the

Berlin subway. It was an upper-class compartment. My eye fell casually on a well-dressed man opposite me, apparently a well-to-do-businessman. . . . I thought idly how well the portly figure of this man fitted into the picture of prosperity which one encountered everywhere in Central Europe in those days: . . . Most of the people were now well dressed and well fed, and the man opposite me was therefore no exception. But when I looked at his face, I did not seem to be looking at a happy face. He appeared to be worried: and not merely worried but acutely unhappy, with eyes staring vacantly ahead and the corners of his mouth drawn in as if in pain—And then I began to look around at all other faces in the compartment—faces belonging without exception to well-dressed, well-fed people: and in almost every one of them I could discern an expression of hidden suffering, so hidden that the owner of the face seemed to be quite unaware of it.

. . . The impression was so strong that I mentioned it to Elsa; and she too began to look around with the careful eyes of a painter accustomed to study human features. Then she turned to me, astonished, and said: "You are right. They all look as though they were suffering torments of hell. . . . I wonder, do they know themselves what is going on in them?"

I knew that they did not—for otherwise they could not go on wasting their lives as they did, without any faith in binding truths, without any goal beyond the desire to raise their own "standard of living," without any hopes other than having more material amenities, more gadgets, and perhaps more power.

... When we returned home, I happened to glance at my desk on which lay open a copy of the *Koran* I had been reading earlier. Mechanically, I picked the book up to put it away, but just as I was about to close it, my eyes fell on the open page before me, and I read:

> You are obsessed by greed for more and more
> Until you go down to your graves.
> Nay, but you will come to know!
> And once again: Nay, but you will come to know!
> Nay, if you but knew it with the knowledge of certainty,
> You would indeed see the hell you are in.
> In time, indeed, you shall see it with the eye of certainty:
> And on that Day you will be asked what you have done
> with the boon of life.[17]

For a moment I was speechless. I think that the book shook in my hands. Then I handed it to Elsa. "Read this. Is it not an answer to what we saw in the subway?"

It was an answer so decisive that all doubt was suddenly at an end. I knew now, beyond any doubt, that it was a God-inspired book I was holding in my hand: for although it had been placed before man over thirteen centuries ago, it clearly anticipated something that could have become true only in this complicated, mechanized, phantom-ridden age of ours.

This, I saw, was not the mere human wisdom of a man of a distant past in distant Arabia. However wise he may have been, such a man could not by himself have foreseen the torment so peculiar to this twentieth century. Out of the *Koran* spoke a voice greater than the voice of Muhammad.[18]

Thus it was that Leopold Weiss became Muhammad Asad. He converted in Berlin before the head of the city's small Muslim community. He took the names Muhammad, to honor the Prophet, and Asad—meaning "lion"—as a reminder of his given name. He took other decisive steps: He broke with his father over his conversion, married Elsa, who also converted, abruptly left his newspaper job, and then set off on pilgrimage to Mecca.

Six years later, after Elsa had died and he had remarried Munira, Asad left Arabia and came to British India. There, in 1932, he met Muhammad Iqbal. Iqbal persuaded Asad to stay in India and help Muslims establish a separate Muslim state. Asad agreed. He remained in British India, where Iqbal encouraged him to translate into English one of the outstanding collections of traditions on the Prophet Muhammad, *Sahih al-Bukhari*. Asad accepted the challenge and completed the work with enthusiasm, but war changed his life. He was arrested in Lahore in 1939, a day after World War II broke out. The British, due to his Austrian background, viewed him as an enemy alien. Asad spent three years incarcerated in a prison; he was not finally released until World War II ended in 1945.

Like Iqbal, and unlike Yusuf Ali, Asad supported the idea of a separate Muslim state in India. After the independence of Pakistan on August 14, 1947, and in recognition for his support of Pakistan, Asad was conferred full citizenship by Pakistan. Although he remained a Pakistani citizen until the end of his life, it was not in Pakistan but rather in Switzerland and then Morocco during the 1960s and 1970s that he was able to dedicate himself to his magnum opus, *The Message of the Qur'an* (1980). He was assisted in this endeavor by his third wife, Pola, a.k.a. Hamida, whom he married in 1952. While his autobiography, *A Road to Mecca* (1954), offers a stunning narrative of bold self-disclosure, it is the originality and scope of his work on the Qur'an that stands apart, both from his other writings and from other efforts to render the Qur'an into English. As one reviewer observed, "in its intellectual engagement with the text and in its subtle and profound understanding of the pure classical Arabic of the *Koran*, Asad's interpretation is of a power and intelligence without rival in English."[19]

What also distinguishes *The Message of the Qur'an* is its rational tone and its pointillist format. It is intended to provide a novel rendition—at once idiomatic and explanatory—of the Qur'anic message into English, even while presenting that message as one marinated in Arabic and only lightly supplemented in English. The long-lasting influence of Muhammad Ali pervades. Consider the first page of the Opening chapter in *The Message of the Quran* (figure 2). The page has four elements:

1. Opposite a page that gives the title in English as the first sura, Al-Fatiha (the Opening), it echoes that name in Arabic, with indication that it was

سورة الفاتحة مكية
وآياتها سبع

IN THE NAME OF GOD, THE MOST
GRACIOUS, THE DISPENSER OF
GRACE:[1] (1)

بِسۡمِ ٱللَّهِ ٱلرَّحۡمَٰنِ ٱلرَّحِيمِ ۝

ALL PRAISE is due to God alone, the
Sustainer of all the worlds,[2] ⟨2⟩ the Most
Gracious, the Dispenser of Grace, ⟨3⟩ Lord
of the Day of Judgment! ⟨4⟩

ٱلۡحَمۡدُ لِلَّهِ رَبِّ ٱلۡعَٰلَمِينَ ۝ ٱلرَّحۡمَٰنِ ٱلرَّحِيمِ ۝ مَٰلِكِ يَوۡمِ

Thee alone do we worship; and unto Thee
alone do we turn for aid. ⟨5⟩

ٱلدِّينِ ۝ إِيَّاكَ نَعۡبُدُ وَإِيَّاكَ نَسۡتَعِينُ ۝ ٱهۡدِنَا ٱلصِّرَٰطَ

Guide us the straight way ⟨6⟩ – the way of
those upon whom Thou hast bestowed
Thy blessings,[3] not of those who have
been condemned [by Thee], nor of those
who go astray![4] ⟨7⟩

ٱلۡمُسۡتَقِيمَ ۝ صِرَٰطَ ٱلَّذِينَ أَنۡعَمۡتَ عَلَيۡهِمۡ غَيۡرِ ٱلۡمَغۡضُوبِ عَلَيۡهِمۡ
وَلَا ٱلضَّآلِّينَ ۝

Bismil-lāhir-Raḥmānir-Raḥīm. ۝
ʾAlḥamdu lillāhi Rabbil-ʿālamīn. ۝ ʾArraḥmānir-
Raḥīm. ۝ Māliki Yawmid-Dīn. ۝ ʾIyyāka naʿbudu
wa ʾIyyāka nastaʿīn. ۝ ʾIhdinaṣ-ṣirāṭal-mustaqīm.
۝ Ṣirāṭal-ladhīna ʾanʿamta ʿalayhim ghayril-
maghḍūbi ʿalayhim wa laḍ-ḍāllīn. ۝

1 According to most of the authorities, this invocation (which occurs at the beginning of every *sūrah* with the exception of *sūrah* 9) constitutes an integral part of "The Opening" and is, therefore, numbered as verse 1. In all other instances, the invocation "in the name of God" precedes the *sūrah* as such, and is not counted among its verses. – Both the divine epithets *raḥmān* and *raḥīm* are derived from the noun *raḥmah*, which signifies "mercy," "compassion," "loving tenderness" and, more comprehensively, "grace." From the very earliest times, Islamic scholars have endeavoured to define the exact shades of meaning which differentiate the two terms. The best and simplest of these explanations is undoubtedly the one advanced by Ibn Qayyim (as quoted in *Manār* I, 48): the term *raḥmān* circumscribes the quality of abounding grace inherent in, and inseparable from, the concept of God's Being, whereas *raḥīm* expresses the manifestation of that grace in, and its effect upon, His creation – in other words, an aspect of His activity.

2 In this instance, the term "worlds" denotes all categories of existence both in the physical and the spiritual sense. The Arabic expression *rabb* – rendered by me as "Sustainer" – embraces a wide complex of meanings not easily expressed by a single term in another language. It comprises the ideas of having a just claim to the possession of anything and, consequently, authority over it, as well as of rearing, sustaining and fostering anything from its inception to its final completion. Thus, the head of a family is called *rabb ad-dār* ("master of the house") because he has authority over it and is responsible for its maintenance; similarly, his wife is called *rabbat ad-dār* ("mistress of the house"). Preceded by the definite article *al*, the designation *rabb* is applied, in the Qur'ān, exclusively to God as the sole fosterer and sustainer of all creation – objective as well as conceptual – and therefore the ultimate source of all authority.

3 I.e., by vouchsafing to them prophetic guidance and enabling them to avail themselves thereof.

4 According to almost all the commentators, God's "condemnation" (*ghaḍab*, lit., "wrath") is synonymous with the evil consequences which man brings upon himself by wilfully rejecting God's guidance and acting contrary to His injunctions. Some commentators (e.g., Zamakhsharī) interpret this passage as follows: ". . . the way of those upon whom Thou hast bestowed Thy blessings – those who have not been condemned [by Thee], and who do not go astray"; in other words, they regard the last two expressions as *defining* "those upon whom Thou hast bestowed Thy blessings". Other commentators (e.g., Baghawī and Ibn Kathīr) do not subscribe to this interpretation – which would imply the use of negative definitions – and understand the last verse of the *sūrah* in the manner rendered by me

FIGURE 2. Chapter 1, Surat al-Fatiha Makkiya (the Opening chapter, Mecca) in Muhammad Asad, *The Message of the Qur'an*. Courtesy of The Book Foundation, United Kingdom

revealed in Mecca (rather than Medina), and that it has seven verses.

2. It gives the Arabic of the initial verse (the *basmala*) in bold letters on the right, with its translation in bold, but less bold, letters and capitalized on the left.

3. Also, in double columns, it gives the remainder of the Arabic text, with transliteration, on the right, mirroring the English translation with each verse enumerated on the left.

4. It provides footnotes on four points deemed crucial to explain how Qur'anic commentators, modern as well as medieval, have reflected on the special qualities of this, the Opening chapter, of the Noble Book, the Holy Qur'an.

Equal stress is placed on the quality and the priority of the Arabic language. Not just the language of the original but also the language *transliterated* is set out, as if to entice the reader, even one who knows no Arabic, to engage with the sounds of the text, or for one familiar with Arabic but not Qur'anic Arabic, to enunciate the Arabic original without error and, through practice, with confidence in its utterance. In other words, it serves not just as a translation but also as a primer for Qur'anic Arabic to be recited.

The major precursor to Asad in prioritizing Arabic even while offering an English translation is Maulana Muhammad Ali. Ali's rendition is less aesthetically charged than Asad's, but it also includes a long commentary on the sources of revelation (*asbab an-nuzul*) and then provides on a single page the Arabic text, the English translation in matching columns, followed by a commentary on multiple features of the original, though Ali, unlike Asad, opted *not* to translate Allah. Figure 3 shows how the initial page of Ali's chapter 1 appears in the seventh edition of *The Holy Qur'an* (figure 3).

One might look at Pickthall and Yusuf Ali as contemporary rivals, which they are since they differ on several points, yet in their determination to prioritize access to the *Koran* in English, they converge with each other, even as they both diverge from Muhammad Ali and Muhammad Asad. It is Pickthall who is the first to prioritize English over Arabic; in his rendition English stands alone, without immediate or direct comparison to the Arabic text of al-Qur'an. This is evident in a sample picture from the same Opening chapter (figure 4).

Yusuf Ali (figure 5), despite his advocacy of English as an Islamic language, seemed initially inclined to follow Muhammad Ali, not Pickthall, as a model for his own translation. The original 1934–37 edition of *The Holy Qur'an: Text, Translation, and Commentary* was published with extensive notes but also with the Arabic text (figure 6). Its full subtitle, while not as lengthy as that of Abdul Majid Daryabadi (see above), safeguarded its connection to the Arabic Qur'an—*The Holy Qur'an: An Interpretation in English, with Arabic text in parallel columns, a running rhythmic commentary in English and full explanatory notes.* Yet from 1957, within four years of the

In[1] the name of Allāh,[2] the Beneficent, the Merciful.[3]   بِسْمِ اللهِ الرَّحْمٰنِ الرَّحِيْمِ ۞

1 Praise be to Allāh, the Lord[5] of the worlds,[6]   اَلْحَمْدُ لِلهِ رَبِّ الْعٰلَمِيْنَ ۞

2 The Beneficent, the Merciful,   الرَّحْمٰنِ الرَّحِيْمِ ۞

3 Master[7] of the day of Requital.[8]   مٰلِكِ يَوْمِ الدِّيْنِ ۞

4 Thee do we serve and Thee do we beseech for help.[8a]   اِيَّاكَ نَعْبُدُ وَاِيَّاكَ نَسْتَعِيْنُ ۞

5 Guide us on[8b] the right path,   اِهْدِنَا الصِّرَاطَ الْمُسْتَقِيْمَ ۞

6 The path of those upon whom Thou hast bestowed favours,[9]   صِرَاطَ الَّذِيْنَ اَنْعَمْتَ عَلَيْهِمْ غَيْرِ

7 Not those upon whom wrath is brought down, nor those who go astray.[10]   الْمَغْضُوْبِ عَلَيْهِمْ وَلَا الضَّآلِّيْنَ ۞

---

1 I retain the ordinary translation of the particle *bā*, but I must warn the reader that the sense of this particle is not the same in Arabic as the sense of the word *in* in the equivalent phrase *in the name of God*. *In*, in the latter case, signifies *on account of*, whereas the *bā* in Arabic signifies *by*, or *through*, or, to be more exact, *with the assistance of*. The phrase is in fact equivalent to: *I seek the assistance of Allāh, the Beneficent, the Merciful* (AH). Hence it is that a Muslim is required to begin every important affair with *Bismillāh*.

2 Allāh, according to the most correct of the opinions respecting it, is a proper name applied to *the Being Who exists necessarily by Himself, comprising all the attributes of perfection* (T-LL), the *al* being *inseparable from it, not derived* (MSb-LL). *Al-ilāh* is a different word, and *Allāh* is not a contraction of *al-ilāh*. The word Allāh is not applied to any being except the only true God, and comprises all the excellent names, and the Arabs never gave the name Allāh to any of their numerous idols. Hence, as being the proper name of the Divine Being and not having any equivalent in any other language, I have adopted the original word in this translation.

3 *Raḥmān* and *Raḥīm* are both derived from *raḥmat*, signifying *tenderness requiring the exercise of beneficence* (R), and thus comprising the ideas of *love* and *mercy*. *Al-Raḥmān* and *al-Raḥīm* are both active participle nouns of different measures denoting intensiveness of significance, the former being of the measure of *faʿlān* and indicating the greatest preponderance of the quality of mercy, and the latter being of the measure of *faʿīl* and being expressive of a constant repetition and manifestation of the attribute (AH). The Prophet is reported to have said: "*Al-Raḥmān* is the Beneficent God Whose love and mercy are manifested in the creation of this world, and *al-Raḥīm* is the Merciful God Whose love and mercy are manifested in the state that comes after". (AH), i.e. in the consequences of the deeds of men. Thus the former is expressive of the utmost degree of love and generosity, the latter of unbounded and constant favour and mercy. Lexicologists agree in holding that the former includes both the believer and the unbeliever for its objects, while the latter relates specially to the believer (LL). Hence I render *al-Raḥmān* as meaning the *Beneficent*, because the idea of doing good is predominant in it, though I must admit that the English language lacks an equivalent of *al-Raḥmān*.

FIGURE 3. Chapter 1 (the Opening) in Muhammad Ali, *The Holy Qur'an*. Courtesy of Aḥmadiyyah Anjuman Ishaʿat Islam Foundation, Lahore, Pakistan

Al-Fâtiḥah, "The Opening," *or Fâtiḥatu'l-Kitâb,* "The Opening of the Scripture" or *Ummu'l-Qurân,* "The Essence of the Koran," as it is variously named, has been called the Lord's Prayer of the Muslims. It is an essential part of all Muslim worship, public and private, and no solemn contract or transaction is complete unless it is recited. The date of revelation is uncertain, but the fact that it has always, from the very earliest times, formed a part of Muslim worship, there being no record or remembrance of its introduction, or of public prayer without it, makes it clear that it was revealed before the fourth year of the Prophet's Mission (the tenth year before the Hijrah); because we know for certain that by that time regular congregational prayers were offered by the little group of Muslims in Mecca. In that year, as the result of insult and attack[1] by the idolaters, the Prophet arranged for the services, which had till then been held out of doors, to take place in a private house.

This sûrah is also often called *Saba'an min al-Mathâni,* "Seven of the Oft-repeated" ("verses" being understood), S. XV, 87, words which are taken as referring to this sûrah.[2]

THE OPENING

Revealed at Mecca

In the name of Allah, the Beneficent, the Merciful.

1. Praise be to Allah, Lord of the Worlds,
2. The Beneficent, the Merciful.
3. Owner of the Day of Judgment,
4. Thee (alone) we worship; Thee (alone) we ask for help.
5. Show us the straight path,
6. The path of those whom Thou hast favoured;
7. Not (the path) of those who earn Thine anger nor of those who go astray.

[1] Ibn Hishâm *Sîrah* (Cairo Ed.), Part 1, p. 88.
[2] See Nöldeke, *Geschichte des Qorâns,* Zweite Auflage, bearbeitet von Fr. Schwally, Part I, pp. 110 *seq.*

TRANSLATOR'S NOTE: I have retained the word Allah throughout, because there is no corresponding word in English. The word *Allâh* (the stress is on the last syllable) has neither feminine nor plural, and has never been applied to anything other than the unimaginable Supreme Being. I use the word "God" only where the corresponding word *ilâh* is found in the Arabic.
The words in brackets are interpolated to explain the meaning.

31

FIGURE 4. Sura 1 Al-Fatiha (the Opening) in Marmaduke Pickthall, *The Meaning of the Glorious Koran*

FIGURE 5. Yusuf Ali (portrait)

author's death, the original Pakistani publisher, Muhammad Ashraf (Lahore), not needing copyright protection, published a separate edition *without* the Arabic texts or appendixes. Several others have since followed that practice, including Amana Publications.

Later, Yusuf Ali's translation, especially in its Amana Publications reprint, became mired in controversy due to the "orthodox" changes imposed by Middle East patrons of American publishers. One does not need to even open the 1996 edition to see the difference from the 1937 original. The Amana title (figure 6) was changed to reflect sensitivity about qualifying its content as "indirect," not "direct" knowledge of the divine source. *The Holy Qur'an* became *The Meaning of the Holy Qur'an*. Yusuf Ali's cosmopolitan background was not only erased; his work was redesigned to project Saudi claims for orthodoxy, claims

FIGURE 6. Cover for the Amana Publications reprint, *The Meaning of the Holy Qur'an*

that were packaged, published, and distributed in millions of Yusuf Ali *Koran* translations (see chapter 6).

Competition about South Asian Translators

The full impact of South Asian scholars in the subsequent history of *Koran* translations into English can only be assessed once we take into account their desire to excel not just in producing a superior work, but also one unlike any other, including and especially the translation of their contemporaries.

It was Muhammad Ali who prepared the way, even as he offered the incentive, for Asad, like others, to make "a really idiomatic, explanatory rendition of the Qur'anic message into English." What has emerged from the South Asian dominance in *Koran* translations is a spectrum of relationships—at once stated and unstated, explicit and discrete—between al-Qur'an, the Arabic Qur'an, and its counterpart, the English *Koran*. At one end, close to the Arabic original is Maulana Muhammad Ali, the original Yusuf Ali, and Muhammad Asad. At the other end of the spectrum, loosening the tether of connection to the original, is Pickthall, the revised Yusuf Ali, and several more recent translators, both Muslim and non-Muslim. Most of the more recent translators, though distant from South Asia, are still influenced by the developments that took place there in forging the English *Koran*.[20]

Ghulam Sarwar foreshadows the complexity of these relationships. While Ghulam Sarwar fully acknowledged the influence of Muhammad Ali, others were more reticent. Asad was probably the most reticent of all. What Asad produced is perhaps the most innovative, far-reaching rendition from the Asian subcontinent. And yet its Asian origins are occluded; in the lengthy introduction to his magnum opus, *The Message of the Qur'an*, Asad never mentions his South Asian predecessors.[21] Elsewhere, however, his association with Pickthall is evident. Asad had been among Pickthall's successors as editor of the prestigious journal *Islamic Culture*, published in Hyderabad, and when Asad published the first edition of his own translation in 1980 he acknowledged Pickthall, though condescendingly: "Pickthall's knowledge of Arabic," he opined, "was limited."[22]

If Asad derided Pickthall, it is because he wanted to be the "first" *Koran* translator. Nor was Asad alone in the quest for primacy as *Koran* translator. What marks all four of these extraordinary translators—Pickthall, Asad, and the two Alis, Yusuf Ali and Muhammad Ali—is the zeitgeist of British, then post-British India: to produce in the language of the Raj a work that would, in Yusuf Ali's words, "make English itself an Islamic language." Each in his own way wanted to be first. In his translator's foreword, Pickthall exults that his "is the first English translation of the *Koran* by an Englishman who is a Muslim."[23] Yusuf Ali strove to make not just a translation but an elevation of the Qur'an for English readers: "The rhythm, music and exalted tone of the original should be reflected in the English interpretation. It may be but a faint reflection, but such beauty and power as my pen can command shall be brought to its service. I want to make English itself an Islamic language, if such a person as I can do it."[24]

On the other hand, for Asad, the role of being first was still greater. In his extensive foreword to the 1980 first edition of *The Message of the Qur'an*,[25] he acknowledges the sincere intent of earlier translators but observes that "none of these translations—whether done by Muslims or by non-Muslims—has so far brought the Qur'an nearer to the hearts and minds of people raised in a different religious and psychological climate and revealed something, however little, of its real depth and wisdom." What is required is more than mere mastery of Arabic through academic study. "In addition to philological learning," he warns, "one needs an instinctive 'feel' of the language." For that reason, in his view, he—and he alone—has produced "an attempt—perhaps the first attempt—at a really idiomatic, explanatory rendition of the Qur'anic message into a European language."

Others have probed the mystery of the Qur'anic message, others have tried to elevate, and register, that mystery in English, but these four, whether from the Asian subcontinent (Muhammad Ali and Yusuf Ali) or influenced by its history (Pickthall and Asad), have set the standard for all subsequent translations of the *Koran* into English.

The Virtual *Koran* and Beyond

CHAPTER 4

A Malaysian Warning

Since the mid-1990s there has been concern in many quarters about the Internet. With the speed and volume of data that it makes possible, there is the difficulty of making a choice about quality. The brave new world is one of endless information and mindless usage of that information. In 1996 Gertrude Himmelfarb observed: "Like postmodernism, the Internet does not distinguish between the true and the false, the important and the trivial, the enduring and the ephemeral." Not surprisingly, the battles over translation and meaning production in English have been mirrored, even magnified, online. As Gary Bunt points out, cyberMuslims have marshaled a variety of resources to prove the validity of certain translations, the unacceptability of others. Yet instead of one dominant site there are "myriad competing sites designed for a variety of readers, ranging from those iMuslims fluent in classical or Qur'anic Arabic to those who have limited knowledge of Arabic or who can only approach the Revelation in a language other than Arabic."[1]

In 1996 I was a Fulbright scholar in Malaysia. I briefly lived and worked in Kuala Lumpur. There was also much discussion about the many new translations of the Qur'an available in English and on the Internet. One article that appeared in the *New Straits Times* announced in its title: "Doubtful Qur'an translations found on the Net." A state official warned: "Some people or groups [mostly from the United States] were translating the Qur'an to suit their own interests and posting them on the Net. [These were] enemies of Islam or Western Orientalists, out to weaken Muslims because they know the source of strength of the Muslims is the Qur'an." To counter this trend, the state official proposed a new strategy: "Pusat Islam [the Malaysian Ministry of Islamic Affairs] has set up a special team of experts to provide correct translations of the Qur'an (into English), and also to promote Qur'an literacy among Muslims in the country."[2]

Luckily the Malaysian minister did not consult the Wikipedia article on Qur'an translations into English. Had he done so, he would have been completely baffled: *Korans* proliferate without any guidepost. The current version (23 January 2017) includes a general history of Qur'an translations into several languages, European, Asian, and African. Despite its capacious overview, the part devoted to English translations feels like a rudimentary catalog with little effort at critical insight. One paragraph cites six early European pioneers, from Robert of Ketton to A. J. Arberry, then four Muslim translators up until 1950 (Abul-Fazl, Muhammad Ali, Pickthall, and Yusuf Ali), followed by a further listing of numerous translators, often focusing on their origin.

N. J. Dawood, for instance, is identified as exceptional for being an Iraqi Jew, and that "explains" his unorthodox translation, while Muhammad Asad is coyly introduced as a Jewish convert to Islam whose "monumental work *The Message of the Qur'an* made its appearance for the first time in 1980." But what makes it monumental? We are never told.[3] Of the Khan-Hilali translation, Wikipedia simply notes that it has Saudi financial backing and "was distributed free worldwide by the Saudi government as it was in line with their particular interpretation." Other items included are either too bizarre or too marginal to be considered as bona fide translations.[4] In short, the Wikipedia entry about English translations of the *Koran* confirms Gertrude Himmelfarb's warning. User beware, a free fall in value awaits the innocent, unsuspecting Internet user.

In a recent effort to summarize the entire spate of *Koran* translations into English, Anthony H. Johns and Suha Taji-Farouki observed: "Many renderings of the Qur'an, both by Muslims and non-Muslims, are simply unreadable: they have no aesthetic appeal, do not communicate the dimension of the Qur'an as a religious text, and in some cases, by straining after effect, make the Qur'anic message appear naïve."[5]

The Case for A. J. Arberry

A notable exception to the above generalization, projecting not only aesthetic appeal but also religious sensibility, is Arthur John Arberry (d. 1969). Better known as A. J.

Arberry, he was a British Orientalist, scholar, translator, editor, and author who wrote, translated, or edited about ninety books on Persian- and Arab-language subjects. Arberry specialized in Sufi studies but is also known for his deft translation of the *Koran*. Many consider *The Koran Interpreted*, which follows in the Pickthall tradition of privileging the host language, English, to be a superior achievement unmatched by any other English translation.

Arberry qualifies as an Orientalist and more. He attended Cambridge University, where he studied Persian and Arabic with R. A. Nicholson, the leading translator of Rumi's *Mathnawi*. After graduation, Arberry worked in Cairo as head of the classics department at Cairo University. During World War II, he took various posts in London to support the war effort with his linguistic skills. In 1944 Arberry was appointed to the chair of Persian at the School of Oriental and African Studies at London University, and then two years later to the chair of Arabic. In 1947 he returned to Cambridge as the Sir Thomas Adams Professor of Arabic, where he remained for over two decades, until his death in 1969.

Arberry himself recounted in an autobiographical sketch how he had come close to losing his Christian faith, even though his family roots were "strict believers of the Christian evangelical school." Paradoxically, his faith was restored following his long in-depth studies of the mystics of Islam. In this regard, commented Arberry, "I am an academic scholar, but I have come to realize that pure reason is unqualified to penetrate the mystery of God's light, and may, indeed, if too fondly indulged, interpose an impenetrable veil between the heart and God. The world is certainly full of shadows. I have had my full share of personal sorrows and anxieties, and I am as acutely aware as the next man of the appalling dangers threatening mankind. But because I have experienced the Divine Light, I need not wish for any higher grace."[6] And in his own engagement with the Qur'anic idiom, one almost senses a surrogate faith, the adamantine Arabic rhythms providing backbone to his own Abrahamic, if dimly Christian, reflexes.

Arberry justifies his new translation as necessary because "a certain uniformity and dull monotony is characteristic of all (others), from the seventeenth century down to the twentieth." Indeed, "in no previous rendering," he asserts, "has a serious attempt been made to imitate, however imperfectly, those rhetorical and rhythmical patterns which are the glory and the sublimity of the *Koran*." His own intent is to do just that: imitate in his Victorian English "those rhetorical and rhythmical patterns which are the glory and the sublimity of the *Koran*."[7] It is perhaps for this reason that *The Koran Interpreted* remains one of the best-selling and most popular English renditions of the Noble Book.

The Best *Korans* Online

There are also several Qur'anic translations available on the Internet that do not conform to the judgment about lack of religious sensibility, even if they are absent aesthetic appeal. Among the most notable translations of the twenty-first century that can be found online is Muhammad Abdel Haleem (2004). Professor of Islamic studies at the School of Oriental and African Studies, London, Abdel Haleem spent years steeped in learning, reciting, studying, and now translating the Qur'an. His is far and away the best seller in English. Prefaced to the translation is an extensive and enlightening overview of things Islamic: articles of faith, history of the revelation, compilation and English translations of the Qur'an and Prophet Muhammad's exemplary life (pp. ix–xxxvi), but what makes this rendition attractive is Abdel Haleem's rendering of the Qur'anic text into refreshingly clear and simple English. Yet his choices tend to reflect traditional, even conservative renderings of most verses, and there is little aesthetic appeal; far from engaging the surplus of poetic sensibility that pervades al-Qur'an, Abdel Haleem makes no effort to match its rhythms with English equivalents.

Equally adroit at seeking an everyday, easeful English for his readers, but also without an effort at "imitating those rhetorical and rhythmical patterns which are the glory and the sublimity of the *Koran*," is Wahiduddin Khan, *The Qur'an: Translation and Commentary with Parallel Arabic Text* (2009). Published in India, it has also been widely disseminated beyond India without the Arabic text (Goodword, 2009). Khan is a prolific, elderly Indian religious leader. A modern-day Gandhian, he has been assisted by two family members in the outreach of his *Koran* translation: his son, Saniyasnain Khan, founded Goodword Books (1996), later coordinated with the Centre for Peace and Spirituality (2001), while his daughter, Fareed Khanam, assisted in his widely disbursed translation (2009). Entering a mosque in Istanbul in 2013, I was surprised to find that the only *Koran* translation available for visitors was Wahiduddin Khan's. It was freely distributed there and is also available online.

Notable among Arab translators is Tarif Khalidi, *The Qur'an: A New Translation* (2008). A professor of Islamic studies at the American University of Beirut, Khalidi had his translation published by Penguin Classics. It is deemed by traditionalists as a worthy counterweight to Orientalist attacks on the Qur'an whether as text, as worldview, or as gender exclusive. Kidwai asserts that Khalidi has spared Islam from further patriarchal attack by Orientalists since he stresses "perhaps the most startling aspect of its [the Qur'anic] rhetoric: the deliberate address to women alongside men, rendering the Qur'an among the most gender-conscious of all sacred texts" (introduction, xvii–xviii). Khalidi also attempts to reproduce the rhythms and distinctive verbal structures of the Arabic text, though his devices often seem contrived; he signals different language visually through a "horizontal" prose presentation of some verses in contrast with a "vertical" poetic layout of others. He does this, he claims, in order to match the source and target languages with parallel "juxtapositions, rhythmic recurrence, sonority, verbal energy and rhymed endings" (xxi). It is widely available online but remains much less popular than Arberry or Abdel Haleem.

There are several other Qur'an translations that are produced online with particular linguistic or national audiences in mind. Two stand out.

A distinctive Persian entry comes from an Indian-born Shiʿi scholar, ʿAli Quli Qaraʾi, *The Qurʾan with a Phrase-by-Phrase English Translation* (2004). Qaraʾi, following the interlinear practice of Persian and Urdu translations of the Qurʾan, hopes that a similar type of phrasal translation will assist English readers. Finding formal equivalence between phrases and clauses in both the source and target texts, in his view, will enable readers to closely follow the meaning of the text. In preparing his rendition he relied on well-known classical commentaries, both Sunni and Shiʿi, but gave special consideration to exegetical traditions transmitted from the *ahl al-bayt*, the family of the Prophet and their successors, the Imams. (It is one of six translations consulted by S. H. Nasr and colleagues in their translation for *The Study Qurʾan* [p. xlii].)

The Turkish counterpoint to Qaraʾi is Ali Unal, *The Qurʾan with Annotated Interpretation in Modern English* (2008). Unal is a member of the Gülen movement, a Turkish Islamic group with broad-gauged appeal not just in Turkey and Central Asia but also throughout Western Europe and North America. Although its tone is progressive and tolerant, the translation itself lacks any rhythmic or elevated tone, while the detailed explanations of most verses relate to the two Turkish doyens of Islamic revivalism: Fethullah Gülen, together with his precursor, Bediuzzaman Said Nursi. It remains to be seen how recent events in Turkey, especially the July 2016 failed coup attempt, implicating Gülen followers both there and abroad, will impact the continued use of Unal's rendition.

Other *Koran*s Online

There are many other works that scarcely register in commercial sales, yet reflect sustained albeit flawed efforts to produce *Koran* translations through collective labor. They include two that are often found online. One is Translation Committee, *The Majestic Qur'an: An English Rendition of Its Meanings* (2000). This massive book was generated by a committee that included Cambridge professor Timothy Winter (Abdal Hakim Murad), the American Muslim writer Uthman Hutchinson, and Mostafa al-Badawi. Supported by the Nawawi Foundation, and published by Starlatch Press, as a handsome bilingual edition, it is no longer available in print. It is also highly derivative. It appears to be little more than the reprint of an earlier committee product: Ali Ozek, N. Uzunoglu, R. Topuzoglu, and M. Maksutoglu, *The Holy Qur'an with English Translation* (Istanbul, 1992), itself largely derived, without acknowledgment, from Pickthall 1930 and Yusuf Ali 1937.

A further collaborative work is Edip Yuksel, with Layth Saleh al-Shaiban and Martha Schulte-Nafeh, *The Qur'an: A Monotheist Translation* (2012). This also is the copy of an earlier work: *The Qur'an—A Pure and Literal Translation* (ca. 2008), but one produced by the same parties. In the first work they are an anonymous group of self-identified progressive Muslims, with avowed intent to make the Qur'an accessible in English and to modern readers, but in the second, recent edition they are identified as Edip Yuksel et al. Of the three websites listed, Free

-minds.org, Brainbowpress.com, Progressivemuslims
.org, only Free-minds.org provides a Kindle edition preview of passages from the 2012 edition.

Online Websites

All the above *Koran* translations can be found online. Increasingly, online websites will dominate traffic in Qur'anic
studies and especially in searches for the multilayered
meaning of the 6,236 verses of the Noble Book. Of the
many online sites, among the best are alim.org, altafsir.org,
tanzil.net, al-quran.info, and islamawakened.com.

Alim.org was founded in 1991 by two software-savvy
South Asian Muslims from Houston, Texas, Shahid
Shah and Amir Jafri. Their goal was to offer online an
educational tool, a social network for Muslims, and a
general purpose portal that provides information about
social services, events, news, and opinion that are of interest to Muslims. They assert that alim.org was "the
first program to combine the powers of Qur'anic translations, commentaries, an extensive subject database,
and a host of other supporting information bases into
one complete cross-referenced program." The range of
translations is small, however. They provide but four:
Asad, Farooq-i Azam Malik, Pickthall, and Yusuf Ali,
and for the last, the rendition is the Saudi-edited version that differs markedly from the original 1937 version. Moreover, the translations of particular verses can
only be compared by a set of consecutive clicks for each

verse on the same page; they cannot be viewed at once on one page.

Altafsir.org was founded a decade later, in 2001, by the Royal Aal al-Bayt Institute for Islamic Thought, Amman, Jordan. It aims to provide "a completely free, non-profit website providing access to the largest and greatest online collection of Qur'anic Commentary (*tafsir* or *tafseer*), translation, recitation and essential resources in the world." Its translations in English, however, are limited to ten: Pickthall, Yusuf Ali, Arberry, and Asad, but also Martin Lings (partial), Muhammad Taqi Usmani, Muhammad Tahir al-Qadri, Sahih International, Laleh Bakhtiar, as well as its own Royal Aal al-Bayt Institute translation. The Royal Aal al-Bayt Institute translation, presented without notes, is clear and idiomatic, though rendition of difficult choices reflects a penchant for Yusuf Ali and/or Pickthall. Moreover, the translations have to be viewed serially from page to page; they cannot be directly compared on the same screen.

Tanzil.net was founded in 2007 by an Iranian computer scientist, Hamid Zarrabi-Zadeh. He heads a team of more than a dozen tech-savvy and well-credentialed Iranian professionals who produce, then monitor the several streams of this website. The one that pertains to Qur'an translation includes seventeen English translations. They can be downloaded one by one or examined in comparison verse by verse: placing the mouse over the Arabic verse, one then indicates which of the several translations one wants to see. While this is a welcome cachet, it is not possible to do side-by-side comparisons of variant translators on a single verse as with alim.org. There is also no rationale as to why some translations were included and others excluded from this website.

Formed in Copenhagen by two scripture-boosting computer scientists, also in 2007, al-quran.info was intended to "improve the way sacred texts are freely studied, compared and recited online." It has an enormous inventory of Qur'an translations in multiple languages, yet one can only compare its forty offerings of English translations in clusters of five. Moreover, the translations themselves are evaluated according to evidence and criteria downloaded from Wikipedia.org in English. Hence we find that Ahmad Zaki Hammad (2007) is commended but never evaluated while Maulana Muhammad Ali (1917) is never mentioned except in his relationship to Shakir (1970). Not only is it odd to have Shakir (1970) included; he is also lauded. Despite evidence of Shakir's dependence on Muhammad Ali and scholarly critique of his proclivity to sectarian bias, this recent effort has been dubbed "a widely used, popular and serviceable translation." Even more surprising is the reference to Thomas Cleary (2004). Though Cleary is praised, his translation is not to be found among the forty listed in English.[8]

Far better than either alim.org, altafsir.org, tanzil.net, or al-quran.info is islamawakened.com. It was started in 2003 by an Anglo convert to Islam, G. Waleed Kavalec. Kavalec works for a Texas-based computer software company, and appropriately he charts his journey to Islam on his Facebook page.[9] He has constructed a site that makes it possible to view no less than fifty-four translations of a single verse simultaneously on the same page. The benefit of this is readily evident when one contrasts the ease of retrieval and clarity of information with what is possible not just on alim.org, altafsir.org, and tanzil.net but also on al-Quran.info. The platform is simple, with each verse entered in Arabic, then transliterated and translated literally. One can scroll down to the first thirty-five entries for each of the 6,236 verses of the Qur'an. These entries are listed as "generally accepted translations of the meaning," and they are followed by ten more that are said to be "controversial, deprecated, or status undetermined works," then a further five categorized as "non-Muslim and/or Orientalist works," while a final four are described as "new and/or partial translations, and works in progress." Even though no commentary is provided on this taxonomy, or particular translations cited within it, the ready reference feature of islamawakened.com exceeds all other competitive websites on *Koran* translations, at least as of 2017.

Recent Translations *Not* Online

Yet the Internet remains a partial resource for locating, and evaluating, *Koran*s in English. There are also several notable recent translations that cannot be found online but deserve mention. The following are the most notable:

1. Thomas Cleary, *The Qur'an: A New Translation* (2004). Cleary is a well-known California-based translator of numerous Buddhist works. This

translation is based on an earlier, partial translation (1993), which was highly praised by the noted American Muslim scholar Hamza Yusuf. Cleary is the sole major translator outside the tradition of either scholarship, affiliation, or linguistic connection to the Muslim world, whether in Africa or Asia, Europe or America, and his work is exceptional for both its minimalism and its creativity. Recently Sandow Birk has mined Cleary in constructing his own hybrid version of the *Koran*, transcribing all 6,236 verses to match the sacred text with visual accents in *American Qur'an* (see chapter 7, "The Graphic *Koran*").

2. Alan Jones, *The Qur'an* (2007). This translation comes from a renowned Oxford University Arabist. Jones's rendering is of particular interest because he is a leading authority on early Arabic poetry. He has used this contextual expertise to develop an approach highlighting the oral/aural structures of Qur'anic Arabic. Jones has given special thought to what the text would have meant to its first hearers. Accordingly, he devises a technique to emphasize the oral origin of the Qur'an's pericopes, one that sets out verses in lines of varying length, indicating the natural points for pause and imitating its rhythmic cadences when recited. The breathtaking originality of Jones's approach, however, is compromised in the view of traditional Muslims by his polemical tone and open critique of received views about Qur'anic origins

and textual integrity.[10] It hovers near the bottom in commercial sales figures for major Koran translations in English.

3. Abdur Raheem Kidwai, *What Is in the Qur'an? Message of the Qur'an in Simple English* (2013). Professor Abdur Raheem Kidwai is an astute reviewer of all prior efforts to render the *Koran* into English. He teaches in the English Department at Aligarh Muslim University, and his own rendition was published by Viva Books, New Delhi, India. It is ironic that one of the most prolific and also insightful of Qur'an translators is not himself available online. Until recently one could download and read his close evaluation of sixty-four translations into English (http://www.Qur'an.org.uk/ieb _Qur'an_untranslatable.htm), but even this resource is no longer available.

4. A. J. Droge, *The Qur'an: A New Annotated Translation* (2013). This is a translation more valued for its scrupulous annotation than for its effective rendition of Arabic into English. Readers will find annotations keyed to the text and divided according to their boldface topical headings at the bottom of each page. While the annotations are not intended to be a commentary, they do provide further information on parallel texts from the Hebrew Bible and also the New Testament. They negotiate some technicalities and also explicate the meaning of obscure passages, though in less detail than *The Study Qur'an* (cited below).

5. William Davut Peachy and Manneh al-Johani, *The Qur'an: The Final Book of God—A Clear English Translation of the Glorious Qur'an* (2012 but not distributed until 2014). This decades-long labor will be discussed in chapter six, "The Politics of *Koran* Translation." The translation differs from others due to its writers' stress on an appeal to native speakers of English. Most other translations are derided as superficial revisions or collations of other well-known translators (p. ix). Although the primary audience of the Peachy-Johani translation is literate, sophisticated English speakers, an important secondary goal is to reach a much wider audience (p. x). They have based their own work on Pickthall's *The Meaning of the Glorious Koran* but with a twist: the predominant aim of the Peachy-Johani translation is to "eliminate the biblical words and modernize the vocabulary of Pickthall's translation" (p. xi). In the introduction, Peachy asserts that their translation has been influenced by Pickthall's approach and wordings, and especially in the introduction of each sura, or chapter, one can detect how Peachy and al-Johani have followed closely Pickthall's style, with only minor difference.

Two More *Koran* Translations

In addition to all the above items, there are two more works, both published to wide acclaim by major publishers, that have not found—nor will likely soon find—their way online:

1. Seyyed Hossein Nasr, *The Study Qur'an*, with Caner K. Dagli, Maria Massi Dakake, Joseph E. Lumbard, and Mohammed Rustom (2015). *The Study Qur'an* is published by the trade publisher HarperOne and designed for mass-market appeal. It is a monumental labor by a team of fifteen scholars working under the renowned polymath Seyyed Hossein Nasr (b. 1933) for nine years (2006–15). Joseph Lombard, the key translator, authors two of the accompanying essays: "The Qur'an in Translation" and "The Qur'anic View of Sacred History and Other Religions." Other essays come from a range of highly regarded authors. They address numerous critical topics, beginning with translation and Qur'an commentary, then extending to science, law, philosophy and theology, mysticism, and art as well as human rights, war and peace, death and dying. There are also appendixes that provide hadith citations, a timeline of Qur'anic events, commentator biographies, along with an index and maps. Nearly 1,200 pages in length, it dwarfs all other efforts in English to provide both a translation and commentary on the Qur'an. Alas, however, the translation is wooden and archaic, only serviceable as a bridge to the commentary.

2. Jane McAuliffe, *The Qur'an* (Norton Critical Editions) (2017). The heralded editor of

Encyclopaedia of the Qur'an (E. J. Brill, 2001–5)
and among the leading Qur'an scholars of her generation, McAuliffe, in her own words, "intends to
use Pickthall's translation as the basic text for this
new Critical Edition since it was just coming out
of copyright. I agreed to the Norton project so
long as I had the latitude to put it into more contemporary English where needed. Pickthall, as you
know, did a solid translation from the Arabic but
tried to give his English rendering an 'elevated'
tone that sounds increasingly archaic to the contemporary ear."[11] McAuliffe's translation bears
comparison to the earlier effort by Arafat K. El-
Ashi (1996/2006), and the more recent effort of
Peachy and al-Johani (2012/2014), both of which
tried to revise, edit, and update Pickthall's translation, averting what one scholar has noted as "the
extremely literal and stiff language of Pickthall."[12]

The Feminist *Koran*?

It is curious that *The Qur'an: A Monotheist Translation*,
cited above, includes a female scholar joining two male
collaborators. It raises the crucial question: are female
scholars/translators of the *Koran* also feminist in their
outlook, method, and goals? The answer is equivocal. Although there are exclusively female endeavors online,
both single- and multiauthored, they do not project a
coherent or holistic agenda that could be touted as

"feminist." Among those works that do give much-needed—and long-delayed—agency to women as *Koran* translators are five oft noted online. Three belong to Saheeh International, *The Qur'an: English Meanings and Notes* (1997), a translation by three American women converts with links to Saudi Arabia, often listed under one Umm Muhammad as the primary author. Projecting their translation online, these three advocate a viewpoint that is consistently conservative, yet on matters like Q 4:34 (see below), they adhere to Yusuf Ali's interpretive stance, translating the final measure against disobedient wives as "strike them [lightly]."[13] The other two are:

1. Tahereh Saffarzadeh, *The Holy Qur'an—Persian and English Translation with Commentary* (bilingual edition, 2006/2011) features an English translation with extensive commentary by the noted Iranian poet, author, and university lecturer. Part of her education was abroad, at the University of Iowa's famed writers' workshop. Having authored ten books on translation theory, she hoped to produce a conceptual translation, with equivalents of the Arabic original in both Persian and English. She could, and did, claim to have produced the first bilingual translation of the Qur'an and the first single-author *Koran* translation into English by a woman. Yet there is no effort to match the rhythmic quality of the Arabic in the target languages; the prose is often stilted, the notes uninspiring, and so the readership outside Iran has

remained close to nil. Published as a hardback book in 2006, it has garnered almost no sales on Amazon.com.[14]

2. Laleh Bakhtiar, *The Sublime Qur'an* (2007). An American Sufi based in Chicago, Laleh Bakhtiar was keen to produce the first English translation of the Qur'an by an American woman.[15] Distinguishing between formal and dynamic equivalence, where the former tries to match the original in the target language and the latter to interpret ideas rather than words, she opts for formal equivalence. Matching word for word, however, too often results in a literalist morass, and even when she succeeds, it is often by imitating the style, or even the wording, of A. J. Arberry (1955).[16] The result is an original but less than arresting feminist rendition of the *Koran* in English.

The Most Contested Verse: Q 4:34

Despite the many differences between the background, approach, and labor of the above women translators, what they share is close attention to verses that highlight the status of women experiencing marital stress, whether domestic discord or actual divorce. Already in Amina Wadud's classic manifesto, *Qur'an and Woman: Reading the Sacred Text from a Woman's Perspective*,[17] how to translate one verse, Q 4:34, became a central issue of contestation. Yusuf Ali's rendition (1937) is still the high-water mark for an inclusive reading of this contro-versial verse:

> *Men are the protectors and maintainers of women*
> *because God has given the one more* [strength] *than the*
>   *other,*
> *and because they support them from their means.*
> *Therefore the righteous women are devoutly obedient,*
> *and guard in* [the husband's] *absence*
> *what God would have them guard.*
> *As to those women on whose part ye fear disloyalty and*
>   *ill-conduct,*
> *admonish them* [first], [Next], *refuse to share their beds,*
> [And last] *beat them* [lightly];
> *but if they return to obedience, seek not against them*
>   *means* [of annoyance]:
> *For God is Most High, Great* [above you all]

The two key terms are *nushuz* (disloyalty and ill-conduct) and *daraba* (to beat—lightly). The most thorough engage-ment with the exegetical issues raised by this verse comes not from a study of *Koran* translations into English, but parallel endeavors into German. They follow Yusuf Ali's intent: to limit the punitive aspect of *daraba*, rendering it as to beat (or better, to strike), but only lightly.[18]

All these endeavors project the constant struggle, amounting to a feminist jihad, to reconcile social justice with scriptural authority in the real as also in the virtual world of the twenty-first century.[19] The debate about Q 4:34, and its key terms, continues to reverberate in the twenty-first century, marking yet another appearance in

Sandow Birk's *American Qur'an*, the subject of chapter seven, below.

Birk is an artist, not a *Koran* scholar, yet he recognizes the fraughtness of this verse. Although his choice for its translation may be without precedent, it is also not far-fetched, either in terms of that verse/chapter or the tone of the Qur'an as a whole.

Here is Birk's rendition:

> Q 4:34 *Men shall take care of women* (Asad) *by what God has given one more than the other, and by what they provide from their property.* (Cleary) *Virtuous women are obedient, careful,* (Rodwell) *who guard the intimacy which God has ordained to be guarded. As for those you have reason to fear rebellion, admonish them, remove them to beds apart, then* <u>restrain them</u>. *And if they obey you, do not seek to harm them.* (Pickthall)

This verse clearly demonstrates the extent to which Birk relies on multiple sources. The initial clause is Asad, but the rest of first sentence is from Cleary (2004), but then he shifts to combine elements from Rodwell and Pickthall though not in any evident pattern: "Virtuous women are obedient, careful" (Rodwell) while the rest follows Pickthall who renders the crucial phrase here as: "good women are the obedient, guarding in secret that which Allah hath guarded. As for those from whom ye fear rebellion, admonish them and banish them to beds apart, and scourge them. Then if they obey you, seek not a way against them."

Rodwell, like Pickthall, uses the word "scourge" to translate *daraba* instead of the more frequent "beat," and Cleary is even stronger: "then spank them." Ignoring his sources, Birk bypasses the troublesome "beat" or "scourge" or "spank" and instead offers the more temperate "restrain" (them). I could find no source which renders *daraba* as restrain, and so I asked Birk about this choice. He volunteered that it was difficult. After consulting with one member of his academic support team, he arrived at "restrain" (them).

Here Birk shows himself to be a careful reader as well as a creative artist. His landmark *American Qur'an* will be discussed in detail in chapter seven, but his wrestling with this fraught passage reveals how he inserts his own understanding of what the Qur'anic message should be: sensitive and supportive, not severe and harmful, to the one being admonished. A bold reinterpretation of the Arabic Qur'an, his wording of Q 4:34 also demonstrates an insight larger than Birk or his other choices in *American Qur'an*: the extent to which all *Koran* translations are at once cumulative, depending on prior choices, and independent, requiring a decision by the individual— whether artist or scholar, believer or unbeliever—on the intended meaning.

The *Koran* Up Close

CHAPTER 5

Why Rhymed Prose Matters

In late 1986 I was in Amman, Jordan. By chance I met a Jordanian academic who had been trained as a scholar of English literature in the United States. Dr. Ibrahim Abu Nab invited me to his home for dinner and conversation. We spent all night talking about just three words. They are the three words that launch the Qur'an. In Arabic, they are: *bismillah ar-rahman ar-rahim*. The first word elides *bismi* with Allah, and hence the whole phrase is known as the *basmala*. The *basmala* begins all but one of the 114 chapters of the Qur'an. We agreed to disagree on the initial name. He opted for Allah, I for God. The latter seemed more resonant to me if the intended audience was native English speakers. "God" over "Allah" is the same choice made by Yusuf Ali, Asad, Peachy, and al-Johani (all Muslims), as well as by Rodwell, Arberry, and Cleary (all non-Muslims). Disagreement on it did not long occupy us that evening. Instead, it was the echo of *rah* in the second and third words that became the heart of our intense conversation. In approaching each word, verse, or chapter of the Qur'an as a translator, argued my host, one must be wary but also hopeful of finding a counterpart in English that echoes the Arabic original.

But how stubborn was the condensed doublet: *rahman/rahim*! What to make in English of these two qualifiers for Allah/God? Was it possible to use a noun, then an adjective in English when the two dependent qualifiers of "Allah/God" in Arabic were both adjectives? In the end, we came out in different places. I preferred to render the Arabic phrase found at the beginning of all but one Qur'anic chapter as: "In the name of God Full of Compassion, ever Compassionate," while he opted for: "In the name of Allah, the Compassion, the Compassionate." To my ear the use of two dependent qualifiers seems closer to the Qur'anic tone than using a noun and an adjective from the same verbal root, or using two adjectives with similar meaning but different verbal roots. The first derived noun qualified Allah, or God, as the One full of compassion. It defines what God is, namely, a reservoir of compassion; God is "*full* of compassion." And the second derived noun acknowledges that the One full of compassion is also marked by a consistent, unending reflex to provide compassion to humankind. The One God who is "full of compassion" is at the same time "ever compassionate."

What united Ibrahim and me was our sense that rhymed prose infused the whole of the Qur'an. We remained in active correspondence until his death in 1991, and though his translation was never completed, its first offerings are available online.[1] The heart of his dedication to the Qur'an was rhymed prose, in English as in Arabic. His mantra became: "The Qur'anic word cannot be stripped of its light, colors and music. Otherwise, it will be reduced to a linear meaning in another language. The word of God will lose its many dimensions; it will become linear flat like the word of man."[2]

Recently, an Iranian German scholar has made a similar plea for opening up study of the Qur'an to the notion of aesthetical, even poetical sensibilities. Recognizing the Qur'anic declarations that Muhammad is not a poet, Navid Kermani agrees, but quickly adds: Muhammad is *not* a poet because he was a poet and something more. He quotes two classical scholars—al-Jāḥiẓ and al-Jurjānī—and also the modern Lebanese poet Adonis on the surplus nature of Muhammad's lyrical eloquence. It was Adonis who exclaimed about the Qur'an: "It is prose, but not like prose; it is poetry, but not like poetry."[3] And by extension, one must search its verses, not its chapters or the text as a whole, for the genuine ecstatic quality of the Noble Book, as the Qur'an is often labeled. Not only is the Qur'an of an aesthetic, musical nature, but its meaning is also inseparable from its sound. To keep meaning intertwined with sound was also the goal of Ibrahim Abu Nab, nowhere more so than in his quest for an appropriate English translation of the *basmala* and all that followed it.

Despite Ibrahim's plea to find "light, colors, and music" in English as in Arabic, most translators ignore the initial clause, as also the remainder of most Qur'anic chapters. The first, or Opening, chapter illustrates the defiant difficulty, and also the recurrent pattern, of those reviewed in earlier chapters. It is especially important to look not just at the Qur'an as a whole but also at individual suras and even more at particular verses. In classical books on the inimitable quality of the Qur'an, "the verse not the *surah* is deemed to be the important unit to examine."[4] And so in what follows I will look at some of the shorter suras, to indicate how pivotal is the sound of their verses in English as a register of meaning, and then conclude by reviewing a pericope or cluster of verses from one of the most defiantly difficult suras to translate, Q 19 Surat Maryam, the chapter on Mary.[5]

All choices made derive from, and are traced back to, the pioneering labor of Maulana Muhammad Ali. If all translators are parasitic, as I argued above, then the identifiable source, or primary root, for Koran translators is this legendary albeit much maligned Ahmadi scholar. I include his rendition, along with three additional translators. Two qualify as "Orientalists" but of very different, contrasting backgrounds. A. J. Arberry, earlier discussed, was probably the most prolific Persian and Arabic translator of the mid-twentieth century. A professor at Cambridge (1947–69), he published his much-acclaimed translation, *The Koran Interpreted*, in 1955. Thomas Cleary has also been a prolific translator, but mostly from Chinese classics. His sole foray into Arabic has been the Qur'an. He published a brief translation, *The Essential Koran* (1993), followed a decade later by *The Qur'an: A New Translation* (2004). Because Cleary's translation of the Opening chapter differed from 1993 to 2004, and also because of his subsequent influence on Sandow Birk (see chapter 7), both are given below. The third translator is Shawkat Toorawa. Like Arberry, Toorawa is at once an esteemed academic and a prolific translator. I have relied on his rhymed translations in much of my own work. Toorawa also resembles Ibrahim Abu Nab: a devout Sunni Muslim and a lifelong Qur'an translator who has yet to complete or publish his own version of the *Koran* in English.[6]

Consider:

1. Muhammad Ali's translation (1917), almost a century ago:

   In the name of Allah, the Beneficent, the Merciful
   1 Praise be to Allah, the Lord of the Worlds,
   2 The Beneficent, the Merciful,
   3 Master of the day of Requital.

2. Pickthall (1930):[7]

   In the name of Allah, the Beneficent, the Merciful
   1 Praise be to Allah, Lord of the Worlds,
   2 The Beneficent, the Merciful,
   3 Sovereign of the Day of Judgment.

3. Yusuf Ali (1934–37):

   1 In the name of God, Most Gracious, Most Merciful
   2 Praise be to God, the Cherisher and Sustainer of
   *   the Worlds;*
   3 Most Gracious, Most Merciful;
   4 Master of the Day of Judgment.

4. A. J. Arberry (1955):

   1 In the Name of God, the Merciful, the
   *   Compassionate*

2 Praise belongs to God, the Lord of all Being,
3 The All-merciful, the All-compassionate,
4 The Master of the Day of Doom.

5. Muhammad Asad (1980/2002):
   1 In the Name of God, the Most Gracious, the
   Dispenser of Grace:
   2 ALL PRAISE is due to God alone, the Sustainer of
   all the worlds,
   3 the Most Gracious, the Dispenser of Grace,
   4 Lord of the Day of Judgment!

6. Cleary 1 (1993):
   1 In the Name of God, the Compassionate, the Merciful
   2 All praise belongs to God,
   Lord of all worlds,
   3 the Compassionate, the Merciful,
   4 Ruler of Judgment Day.

7. Cleary 2 (2004):
   1 In the name of God,
   the Benevolent,
   the Merciful
   2 Praise is proper to God,
   Lord of the universe.
   3 the Benevolent,
   the Merciful,
   4 Ruler of the Day of Requital.

8. And finally Toorawa:
   1 In the Name of God, Ever Compassionate, Full of
   Compassion

2 Praise to the Lord of all Creation,

3 Ever Compassionate, Full of Compassion,

4 Sovereign of the Day of Determination.[8]

The clearest contrast is within Cleary. Both in language and format, his two versions could not provide a stronger contrast of style and outcome. "The Compassionate" is stronger than "the Benevolent" as a measure of *rahman*, though both require a matching qualifier in *rahim*; and none is given in either case. While "Lord of the universe" is better than "Lord of both worlds," both "Ruler of the Day of Requital" and "Ruler of Judgment Day" seem labored, especially compared to Asad: "Lord of the Day of Judgment."

Yet each translator has an approach that dictates the choice of words and patterns. None is determined by allegiance to Islam, or to "orthodox" Islam. While Arberry and Cleary have no frame introduction or commentary or notes, neither does Toorawa, except for an explanation of his rhyme reversal. It is the central notion of what counts in the exchange between the source and target languages that distinguishes each translator.[9] Muhammad Ali sets the tone for what can be called the "theatrical" approach, staging each chapter with elements that announce its message and then detail the central elements of that message:

PART 1[10]

CHAPTER 1

Al-Fatihah: THE OPENING

(REVEALED AT MAKKAH: 7 verses)

In his own translation of the Opening, Pickthall stays very close to Muhammad Ali, even using the variant verse order in earlier editions. In other words, he does not count the initial *basmala* as a verse (which happens only here in the entire Arabic Qur'an), but instead parses the final clause about "the path" into two verses, rather than the single verse found elsewhere. Common to all translations is the insistence that *Al-Fatihah* must be seven verses, but only Muhammad Ali and early Pickthall of major translators fail to count the *basmala* as a verse.[11]

These observations about translation protocol and the overlap between translators are confirmed when a few other sample selections are examined, and none stretch the spectrum of comparison further than the final three suras or chapters: 112, 113, 114. All are short, but also illustrative of the choices that each translator has to make. Here are the choices of the two Alis (Muhammad and Yusuf), the two Clearys (1993, 2004), and Toorawa.

    1. Muhammad Ali:[12]

       CHAPTER 112 *Al-Ikhlas*: THE UNITY

       In the name of Allah, the Beneficent, the Merciful
       1 Say: He, Allah, is One.
       2 Allah is He on Whom all depend.
       3 He begets not, nor is He begotten;
       4 And none is like Him.

       CHAPTER 113 *Al-Falaq*: THE DAWN

       In the name of Allah, the Beneficent, the Merciful

1 Say: I seek refuge in the Lord of the dawn,
2 From the evil of that which He has created,
3 And from the evil of intense darkness, when it comes,
4 And from the evil of those who cast (evil suggestions)
in firm resolutions,
5 And from the evil of the envier when he envies.

CHAPTER 114 *Al-Nas*: THE MEN

In the name of Allah, the Beneficent, the Merciful
1 Say: I seek refuge in the Lord of men,
2 The King of men,
3 The God of men,
4 From the evil of the whisperings of the slinking (devil),
5 Who whispers into the hearts of men,
6 From among the jinn and the men.

2. Abdullah Yusuf Ali:

Surah 112 Al-Ikhlas: *Purity of Faith*

In the name of God, Most Gracious, Most Merciful
1 Say: He is God, the One and Only;
2 God, the Eternal, Absolute;
3 He begetteth not, nor is He begotten.
4 And there is none like unto Him.

Surah 113 Al-Falaq: *The Daybreak*

In the name of God, Most Gracious, Most Merciful
1 Say: I seek refuge with the Lord of the Dawn
2 From the mischief of created things;
3 From the mischief of Darkness as it overspreads;
4 From the mischief of those who practise secret arts;

*5 And from the mischief of the envious one as he
    practises envy.*

Surah 114 An-Nas: *Mankind*

In the name of God, Most Gracious, Most Merciful.
*1 Say: I seek refuge with the Lord and Cherisher of
    Mankind*
2 The King (or Ruler) of Mankind,
3 The God (or judge) of Mankind—
*4 From the mischief of the Whisperer (of Evil), who
    withdraws (after his whisper)—*
5 (The same) who whispers into the hearts of Mankind—
6 Among Jinns and among Men.

Now observe the shift in Cleary's choices:

3. Cleary 1 (1993)

   PURE TRUTH

   In the name of God, Most Gracious, Most Merciful.

   Say, "It is God, Unique,
   God the Ultimate.
   God does not reproduce
   and is not reproduced.
   And there is nothing at all
   equivalent to God."

4. Cleary 2 (2004)

   112. Pure Truth

   In the name of God, the Benevolent, the Merciful
   1 Say, "It is God, unique

2 *"God the eternal,*
3 *"not begetting or begotten,*
4 *"not having any equal."*

Just as we see the shift from "Ultimate" to "Eternal," from reproduce/d to begetting/begotten in Cleary's two versions of Q 112, so there are similar contrasts between Cleary's two renditions for the final two chapters of the *Koran.* While it is strange that he does not number the chapters in his first book, that is likely due to its introductory, popular tone as *The Essential Koran.* The translation is more problematic in the second than in the first rendition of each of these chapters. Not only does he shift from "compassionate" to "benevolent" in the *basmala,* but he seems to lose his way in rendering "evil" as "ill," a drastic de-metaphysical reading of what are often used as apotropaic texts.

THE DAWN (1993)

In the Name of God, the Compassionate, the Merciful

Say, "I take refuge
in the Lord of the dawn
from the evil
of what it created,
and from the evil
of darkness when it is encompassing,
and from the evil
of cursers,
and from the evil of the envious
when they envy."

113. Dawn (2004)

In the name of God, the Benevolent, the Merciful

1 Say, "I take refuge in the Lord of dawn
2 "from the ill of what is created,
3 "and from the ill of darkness when it's gloomy,
4 "and from the ill of those who curse,
5 "and from the ill of the envious when he envies."

Humankind (1993)

In the Name of God, the Compassionate, the Merciful

Say,
"I take refuge
in the Lord of humankind,
the Ruler of humankind,
the God of humankind,
from the evil of insidious suggestion
that whispers in human hearts
from demonic and human sources."

114. Humankind (2004)

In the name of God, the Benevolent, the Merciful

1 Say, "I take refuge with the Lord of humankind,
2 "the ruler of humankind,
3 "the God of humankind,
4 "from the ill of flighty suggestion
5 "that whispers in people's hearts
6 "from demonic and human sources."

Much more consistent in his strategy, as also in his hinging of verses from one sura to another and echoing "mischief" (Q 113) from Yusif Ali, is what we find in:

5. Shawkat Toorawa[13]

112. Purity of Faith

In the Name of God, Full of Compassion, Ever
    Compassionate
1 Affirm: He is God, Matchless
2 God, Ceaseless,
3 Unbegetting, Birthless,
4 Without a single partner, Peerless.

113. The Dawn

In the Name of God, Full of Compassion, Ever
    Compassionate
1 Repeat: "I seek refuge in the Lord of the dawn,
2 From the mischief of His Creation,
3 And from the mischief of night gloom when it blots,
4 And from the mischief of sorceresses, spitting on knots,
5 And from the mischief of the envious envier, when he
    plots."

114. Humanity

In the name of God Full of Compassion, Ever
    Compassionate
Repeat: I seek protection with the Lord of Creation
the King of Creation
the God of Creation

From the malicious incantations
Of the Accursed, whispering insinuations
In the hearts of jinn and humankind both, fabrications.

Q 114

Toorawa, and Toorawa alone of the above major translators, seeks to provide an end line rhyme in each sura for
each verse. He is rapt in his attention to sound as integral
to, and inseparable from, meaning. It is as if he is seeking
to evoke what Arberry had called "those rhetorical and
rhythmical patterns which are the glory and the sublimity of the *Koran*."[14]

If I seem to be preferring Toorawa's strategies and his
choices, it is because they seem consistently attentive to
the performative and auditory dimensions of Qur'an
translation. Although many have written and argued
about *saj'*, the Qur'an's cadenced rhyming prose, almost
no one has shown how it works in the actual labor of
those who translate the *Koran* into English. Mindful of
long-standing critiques directed at every effort to translate the "meaning" of the Qur'an, I will evaluate the professional efforts of three translators—Yusuf Ali and
Toorawa (Muslims) with Habib and Lawrence (Muslim–
non-Muslim)[15]—in light of their attention to cadenced
rhyming prose. In order to sharpen the comparison between these translators, and also to evaluate their competing arguments regarding *saj'*, I will restrict myself to
five verses from one sura: Surat Maryam. These are emotive verses, focusing, as they do, on Mary's perplexity and
anxiety at the role into which she is being cast:

1. Yusuf Ali (1937 original):

   16 Relate in the Book (the story of) Mary, when she withdrew from her family to a place in the East.

   17 She placed a screen (to screen herself) from them; then We sent her our angel, and he appeared before her as a man in all respects.

   18 She said: "I seek refuge from thee to (God) Most Gracious: (come not near) if thou dost fear God."

   19 He said: "Nay, I am only a messenger from thy Lord, (to announce) to thee the gift of a holy son."

   20 She said: "How shall I have a son, seeing that no man has touched me, and I am not unchaste?"

   21 He said: "So (it will be): Thy Lord saith, 'that is easy for Me: and (We wish) to appoint him as a Sign unto men and a Mercy from Us': It is a matter (so) decreed."

2. Shawkat Toorawa[16]

   16 Recall Mary in the Scripture, when she withdrew from her people to a place easterly.

   17 She placed a screen between them and her. Then We sent her Our Spirit, who appeared to her as a man, formed fully.

   18 She said, "I seek refuge from you with the Lord of Mercy! Away, if you have true piety!"

   19 "I am a only a messenger from your Lord," he said, "come to bestow a on you a son of great purity."

   20 "How can I have a son," she asked, "when no man has touched me and I have not engaged in harlotry!"

21 "It shall be so!" he said. "Your Lord says, 'It is easy
for Me!—We shall make him a Sign for people and
a Mercy from Us.'" This is a firm decree.

3. Habib and Lawrence (2019)

16 And mention in the Book
Mary, of when she withdrew herself
from her people
to a place in the East.
17 She veiled herself
from them. Then We sent
Our spirit, appearing
to her fully
in the form of a man.
18 She said: "I seek refuge
with the All Merciful
from you, [withdraw]
if you fear Him."
19 He said: "I am only
a messenger of your Lord,
granting you a pure son."
20 "How shall I
have a son," she said, "for
no man has touched me,
nor have I been unchaste?"
21 He said: "This is what
your Lord has said:
'Easy it is for Me; We
will make him
a sign for humankind,

and a mercy from Us.
It is a thing
ordained.'"

What is important to recognize is not just the translation strategy—how to introduce rhyme and rhythm into English that echoes the original Arabic—but also how to frame the visual flow of words in print for English readers. The overriding purpose is to engage the reader as a reciter. In the same way that the original Qur'an was a spoken not a written text, the feel of its English equivalent must goad the reader to speak out loud, to announce, and then repeat the words that appear on a page. In this sense, Toorawa hits on the final end rhyme as the hook that will keep the reader/reciter engaged in the flow of the Arabic text from beginning to end. Habib and Lawrence share the same goal with Toorawa but follow another trajectory: to mark the flow of words through a hesitation or pause after each line, in order to capture the full tone—the emotion as well as the meaning—of the entire verse. Both endeavors seek to expose what Navid Kermani, echoing the eleventh-century scholar al-Jurjānī, depicts as "the explosive power of each verse of the Qur'an."[17] The strategy is to appeal to the full spectrum of sound/meaning, to draw from each fragment/sign/verse a sense of the whole that engages, elevates, and motivates the listener. In both cases there is attention to the aesthetic aura of the Qur'an not merely to the literal rendition of its original meaning. No translator or translation has succeeded in that endeavor, making the "perfect" or even the "near perfect" rendition of the *Koran* in English, a goal as elusive as it is desirable.

Often the efforts of numerous well intentioned individuals are thwarted, or distorted, by forces beyond their control. It is the interference of political actors, with institutional and nationalist agendas, that concerns us in the next chapter. The most rigorously puritanical custodian of Sunni orthodoxy occupies center stage: the Kingdom of Saudi Arabia.

The Politics of *Koran* Translation

CHAPTER 6

The Saudi Juggernaut

It was February 2008. I had traveled to Saudi Arabia to attend the annual meeting of the Jeddah Economic Forum. When I checked in to my hotel, I found in my bedside cabinet a copy of the Qur'an. It was a huge edition in Arabic and English. It was the Khan-Hilali version. Anyone who has traveled, whether in the United States or abroad, has found in their nightstand a copy of some scriptural text, Bible, Qur'an, or (in India) the Bhagavad Gita. It was not unexpected to find a copy of the Qur'an in a Saudi hotel, but why the Khan-Hilali version? The answer circles back to the King Fahd Complex for Printing the Holy Qur'an (figure 7). Named after King Fahd bin Abdul Aziz Al-Saud (d. 2005), the center of Saudi orthodoxy was established in Medina in 1984, under the Ministry of Islamic Affairs.

Its goal was to promote the Qur'an worldwide. It has the means to do so. Staffed with more than 2,000 employees, the King Fahd Complex for Printing the Holy Qur'an produces about ten million copies of the Qur'an

FIGURE 7. King Fahd Complex for Printing the Holy Qur'an

each year, distributing them within and beyond the Kingdom of Saudi Arabia.[1] As of summer 2015 it had produced and distributed 286 million copies of the Qur'an. Although it is impossible to know how many of those include the Qur'an in translation, and further in English translation, there have been *Meanings* of the Holy Qur'an rendered into more than twenty languages, with English the largest target.[2] In many ways it is the Sunni Muslim counterpart to Protestant Christian Bible societies, for although Shi'i Muslims produce and disseminate copies of the Qur'an, they, like their Catholic counterparts in Christianity, place less emphasis on direct access to canonical scripture. The King Fahd Complex for Printing the Holy Qur'an not only produces, it also monitors access to, and study of, the central scripture of Islam. Of the more than sixty editions of the Qur'an that have appeared since 1984, all those in English invariably follow the template of providing a commentary on the Arabic text (the model of Muhammad Ali and original Yusuf Ali) rather than a free-standing English text (the model of Marmaduke Pickthall and revised Yusuf Ali as also numerous others).

There has been, and remains, internal debate about which translation to use. Initially, the complex embraced a modified version of Yusuf Ali's 1937 translation, which, as noted earlier, ceased to be under copyright after the author's death in 1953. As early as 1980, the Saudi religious establishment felt the need for a reliable English translation and exegesis of the Qur'an, one that could service the rapidly expanding English-language readership of Muslims in Europe, America, and also Asia and Africa. After surveying the various translations in print at the time, four high-level committees recommended Yusuf Ali's translation and commentary as the best that was available. No reason was ever given why Pickthall or some other translator was not selected, but significant revisions were made in the original Yusuf Ali translation before it was printed in 1985 by the King Fahd Complex for Printing the Holy Qur'an. For the next decade this edition served as the officially sanctioned English translation of the Saudi religious establishment.

In the huge North American market, the modified Yusuf Ali translation almost at once established its preeminent position. Amana Publications had reprinted the original edition in 1977, retitling it as *The Meaning of the Holy Qur'an* (see chapter 3, figure 4). At first printed in paperback in two volumes, it was consolidated into a single hardback edition in 1983, and then, once embraced by Saudi officialdom, Amana introduced in 1989 a revised "New Fourth Edition" featuring both revision of the translation and reduction of the commentary. The new revised Amana edition is currently in its eleventh printing, dating back to May 2004, and it remains a best seller.[3]

What replaced Yusuf Ali in 1995 was the independent effort by two non-Saudi scholars who had worked in the Kingdom and become Saudi citizens. Dr. Muhammad Taqiuddin al-Hilali was a traditional Islamic scholar from Morocco who had earned his PhD in Berlin and then taught in several countries, including India, before becoming an Islamic studies professor in the Islamic University at Madinah. His collaborator, Dr. Muhammad Muhsin Khan, was a Pakistani physician who had trained in the United Kingdom and then moved to Saudi Arabia where he served as a physician first in Taif and later at the Islamic University at Madinah. Proficient in Arabic, he worked in the late 1960s to translate one of the major collections of hadith (the Sahih of Bukhari), and it was Dr. Hilali who read, corrected, and revised that translation. Together they began working on the Qur'an.

Khan and Hilali published preliminary versions of their joint *Koran* translation in the 1970s but kept revising the text until they completed two versions, one estimated to be nine volumes in length, the other a summary of less than 800 pages titled *Interpretation of the Meanings of the Noble Qur'an in the English Language: A summarized version of al-Tabari, al-Qurtubi, and Ibn Kathir with comments from Sahih al-Bukhari.* It was this summary, published in 1993 by Maktaba Dar al-Salam in Riyadh, that became the standard text of the Fahd Complex. As one Muslim reviewer noted a decade ago, about Khan-Hilali is

> now the most widely disseminated Qur'an in most Islamic bookstores and Sunni mosques throughout the English-speaking world, this new translation is meant to replace the Yusuf Ali edition and comes with a seal of approval from both the University of Medina and the Saudi *Dar al-Ifta*. Whereas most other translators have tried to render the Qur'an applicable to a modern readership, this Saudi-financed venture tries to impose the commentaries of Tabari (d. 923 C.E.), Qurtubi (d. 1273 C.E.), and Ibn Kathir (d. 1372 C.E.), medievalists who knew nothing of modern concepts of pluralism. The numerous interpolations make this translation particularly problematic, especially for American Muslims who, in the aftermath of 9-11, are struggling to show that Islam is a religion of tolerance.
>
> From the beginning, [the reviewer notes] the Hilali and Muhsin Khan translation reads more like a supremacist Muslim, anti-Semitic, anti-Christian polemic than a rendition of Islamic scripture. In the Opening *sura*, for example, verses which are universally accepted as, "Guide us to the straight path, the path of those whom You have favored, not of those who have incurred Your wrath, nor of those who have gone astray" become, "Guide us to the Straight Way, the way of those on whom You have bestowed Your

Grace, not (the way) of those who have earned Your anger (such as the Jews), nor of those who went astray (such as the Christians)." What is particularly egregious about this interpolation is that it is followed by an extremely long footnote to justify its hate based on traditions from medieval texts.[4]

Alternative Saudi *Koran*s

Perhaps the most detrimental aspect of Saudi supervision of *Koran* translations is not only what is included but also what is excluded or marginalized. Not all dark matter is destined to be dark; not all *Koran* translations lack merit, but beyond the filter of orthodoxy they do not easily find audiences and spur engagement with the Qur'anic message. The above-cited Muslim reviewer is sympathetic to Muhammad Asad's *The Message of the Qur'an*. Yet he observes: "Indicative of the desire and drive of Saudi Arabia to impose a Salafi interpretation upon the Muslim world, the kingdom has banned Muhammad Asad's work over some creedal issues. Because the Saudi government subsidizes the publication and distribution of so many translations, the ban has in effect made Asad's translation both expensive and difficult to obtain."[5] Ironically, however, an independent Saudi sponsor, the Book Foundation, has underwritten the republication of Asad, with the handsome calligraphy of Ahmed Moustafa, since 2003, giving it considerable visibility among global Islam watchers if not the average mosque goer.[6]

Less fortunate in finding alternative means of sponsorship and distribution has been Al-Johani and Peachy, *The Qur'an: The Final Book of God—A Clear English Translation of the Glorious Qur'an* (Qassim, Saudi Arabia: World Assembly of Muslim Youth, 2012). Soon after its publication, one enthusiastic review pronounced: "It can be undoubtedly assumed that Peachy and Al-Johani's effort clearly validates and rationalizes their translation's title, and justifies their claim to publish the best and the most accurate translation which is thoroughly capable of conveying the meaning and the message of the Qur'an. Among all of the published English translations of the Qur'an since 2000, *The Qur'an: The Final Book of God—A Clear English Translation of the Glorious Qur'an* is unique in many ways and indeed stands apart from others."[7]

Yet rarely does one even find mention of this "new" translation. It is not offered on Amazon.com or on any Islamic bookseller webpage. The reasons go back to the unusual commitment of the two collaborators: Peachy was an American convert, al-Johani, a progressive Saudi scholar. Here is how Peachy explains the dilemma they faced:

It is very important to think about for whom we are translating. The English which is used today did not exist 1400 years ago. The first English translations are very difficult to understand today. For example, Abdullah Yusuf Ali was a British-Indian Islamic scholar who translated the Qur'an into English.

... When I started my translation with my partner, the late Dr Maneh Hammad Al-Johani, we had decided to translate in a clear and understandable way. My native language is English and his mother tongue was Arabic. When we came to disagreement, we consulted interpretations and scholars. We worked together for 10 years. After his death in a traffic accident, I continued to work another 10 years. It was finally published 3 years ago (in 2012). Nevertheless, there was one audience we neglected to consider. That was the authorities of Saudi Arabia, namely the Ministry of Religious Affairs. *They wanted to stick to their own old translation because our translation did not commit to one interpretation of the Qur'an.* In the end, it [that old translation] pleased the officials of the Saudi Arabian State, but most Muslims find it ugly. Therefore, the audience is very important.[8]

Alas, in the near future, there will be little, if no, audience for *The Qur'an: The Final Book of God—A Clear English Translation of the Glorious Qur'an.* Intrigued by its 2013 review, I tried and failed to purchase it online. When I wrote the author about my frustration, he sent me a copy. I then met him in Turkey, where he now lives, in fall 2014. We had an extended conversation about *Koran* translation. On two points he was firm: (1) the English text had to stand on its own merits, apart from not next to the original Arabic; and (2) key terms like Allah and *islam* had to be translated, Allah as God and *islam* as surrender.[9] His manner was sincere, direct, humble, and frank. Peachy, working without his Saudi collaborator for over a decade, has accepted that Saudi authorities, even after having agreed to publish his book, will not now distribute it "because it did not commit to one interpretation of the Qur'an." He is hoping to find an alternative route of publication in Turkey, but his case demonstrates graphically how pervasive is Saudi control over Qur'anic meanings and how tortuous is the path to accessibility rather than orthodoxy in advocating *Koran* translation.

Commercial Favorites

The major contenders for the large market in *Koran* translations are likely to be S. H. Nasr (2015) for academics, and Abdel Haleem (2004) for most readers. The Nasr work is a hefty 1,000-plus pages with far more commentary than translation, while Abdel Haleem is the reverse: sparse on interpretive notes, it tries to present Qur'anic Arabic in contemporary, if prosaic, English. One of the attractions of Abdel Haleem is its availability in Oxford Islamic Studies Online, where it is accessed with more frequency than other translations available online. Penguin, eager to be a player in *Koran* translation sales, moved from Dawood to Khalidi, but it is not clear that the payoff is what they expected. Norton also has two other projects that will keep it in *Koran* translation sweepstakes: (1) Sandow Birk, *American Qur'an*[10] and (2) Jane McAuliffe, *The Qur'an* (Norton Critical Editions). There is also the Liveright project, involving myself and Professor Rafey Habib. Titled *The Qur'an: A Verse Translation*, it is not due to be completed until 2019.

One crucial audience in marketing *Koran* translations is the next generation of American college students. What have been the tactics for expanding an interest in the English *Koran* among university undergraduates? A major event was the assignment of Michael Sells's *Approaching the Qur'an: The Early Revelations* (1999/2001) to a freshman reading class at the University of North Carolina in fall 2002. Sells is a renowned scholar of Arabic literature and Islamic culture, and his book offers a high-water mark of creative engagement with the Qur'anic text in its first disclosure (610–22). Conservative protests in North Carolina actually broadened the national appeal of Sells's innovative work, not least through its accompanying CD: it offers the call to prayer (*adhan*) along with eight recitations of selected Qur'anic chapters. It remains the preferred text for many introductory courses on either Islam or the Qur'an. Both the scandal and its aftermath have been well charted.[11]

Competing with the progressive and linguistic approach of Sells is another declamatory, "orthodox" voice. Its message has often been channeled through Muslim Students Associations (MSAs). Whether through actual or virtual networks, they have tended to promote the Saudi-approved translations—first Yusuf Ali adapted, then the Khan-Hilali substitute, followed by another version of Yusuf Ali. The impact of neo-Salafi translations can easily be traced online at several sites. All are aimed at MSA audiences.[12] Ironically, the weight of neo-Salafi conservatism could not be broken even with the best entry for conservatives who are also progressives, that of Peachy-Johani, discussed above.

The Role of Popular Media

Although claiming to be above the fray in assessing all endeavors to engage the *Koran*, popular media, in the United States even more than the United Kingdom, are prone to repeat any charges that declaim the *Koran*, including its status as a book worthy of attention in English translation as also in the original Arabic. Consider Toby Lester, "What Is the *Koran*?" A two-part article published in the *Atlantic Monthly* well before 9/11,[13] it became a reference point for other endeavors not so much to understand the *Koran* as to point out its foreignness, its alien resistance to biblical themes or Western values. Even those who seem to salute the *Koran* as a challenging but bracing read, find in the end that they must disagree with its tenets in order to maintain their own neutrality. Hence Garry Wills, a nimble Catholic scholar, wrote a piece in the *New York Review of Books* sixteen years after Lester's essay. It was titled "My *Koran* Problem." While there is elevated discussion of several issues in that essay, toward the end Wills declares: "I do not want to make my attempts at understanding the *Koran* become an apologia for it. I am repelled by some aspects of the book— the acceptance of slavery, of polygamy, of patriarchy, of war—but I take heart from the fact that many Muslims are repelled by these things too. After all, there is slavery, polygamy, patriarchy, and war in the Old Testament—and Jews have even more reason to be repelled by that than I do. To understand others' religion is to empathize with the problems he or she has concerning it. Religion is a dangerous thing—like sex, and love, and marriage."[14] And so all religion remains dangerous, with Islam still trapped by the three bugbears of premodernity—slavery, polygamy, and patriarchy—while also pursuing the Jewish, Christian, and also secular proclivity for war. It is not a happy picture, nor does it provide a positive incentive to read the *Koran*.

Unlike the above provocateurs, the Ismaili Institute in London is a further major player mounting a sustained effort to diversify and pluralize Qur'an interpretation as the heart of new thinking, scholarship, and advocacy regarding the *Koran* in English. It may not reverse the tide of negativity, common alike to much scholarship and public readings of the *Koran*, but it does offer a new vista of understanding. While they have produced no translation, the spate of literature concerning *Koran* translations has been enormous. A few deserve special mention: Brett Wilson, *Translating the Qur'an in an Age of Nationalism: Print Culture and Modern Islam in Turkey* (2014), Suha Taji-Farouki, ed., *The Qur'an and Its Readers Worldwide: Contemporary Commentaries and Translations* (2016), and multiple works authored or edited by the foremost German scholar of the Qur'an, Angelika Neuwirth, in English.[15]

Finally, one cannot provide an overview of publishing companies and their role in promoting, then disseminating *Koran* translations without considering the Penguin saga. It features N. J. Dawood and his Penguin-published rendition of the Qur'an: *The Koran* (1956). Kidwai mentions it in reviewing Tarif Khalidi (2008). Less than two pages in length, the entire first part of the review is devoted to criticizing N. J. Dawood, whose translation had previously been published by Penguin. Penguin obviously agreed with Arberry, who had praised it, and reissued Dawood's 1956 translation in 1964 as part of its World Classics series. The role constituted for the translator here is that "of purveyor of a literary masterpiece." Why then did Penguin shift from Dawood to Kahlidi, whose translation Penguin published in 2008? In part, at least, to deflect attention from Dawood as a Jewish translator, but that anti-Semitic slur also appears to be just a thinly disguised variation of the recurrent charge that *any* non-Muslim scholar is unable or unwilling to consider the true meaning of the Qur'an. It is a charge multiply refuted by several worthy and lauded translators noted above. The latest rejoinder to that charge is not a translator per se but a transcriber of multiple translations who is also an illuminator of the *Koran*. It is to Sandow Birk and his *American Qur'an* that I now turn to explore the latest, as also the most creative, effort to project the *Koran* in stand-alone English without Arabic adornment.

The Graphic *Koran*

CHAPTER 7

From Asad to Birk

In the previous pages, I have surveyed the circuits of labor that struggle to translate the untranslatable. With the Orientalist *Koran*, the South Asian *Koran*, the Virtual *Koran*, as also the *Koran* Politicized, I have examined strategies to make the sacred text accessible to a variety of audiences. Diverse are the motives, and often disparate are the outcomes, for those who attempt to translate ancient Arabic into modern English. The emphasis is often on literary strategies, engaging the source and target languages, whether from within or beyond the confines of orthodoxy, and cultural bias.

The partial exception comes from Asad. Asad's original translation was modestly bilingual. The 1980 edition, published by Dar Al-Andalus (Gibraltar), featured a chaste cover in green and gold, but the 2003 edition from the Book Foundation (United Kingdom), linked to the Alireza family of Jeddah, Kingdom of Saudi Arabia, offered a sumptuous new format that was more heavily Arabicized than its predecessor. Not only did it include the

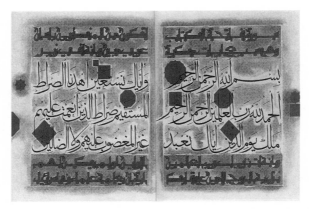

FIGURE 8. Ahmed Moustafa calligraphy of Fatiha in Muhammad Asad, *The Message of the Qur'an*

feature of transliteration, providing for each chapter and verse transliteration as well as translation of the Qur'anic Arabic, but it also displayed the Ka'ba announcing the *basmala* on its cover.

Prominent signature calligraphic folios adorned various parts of the Arabic text, beginning with one that preceded sura Al-Fatiha (Q 1). The calligrapher who provided the Ka'ba cover as well as all the calligraphic highlights is Ahmed Moustafa (figure 8). An Egyptian artist trained in the United Kingdom and now based in London, Moustafa has marketed his calligraphy apart from its representation in *The Message of the Qur'an*, yet his calligraphic inserts in the 2003 Jeddah edition of Asad's translation place it in a category remote from any other *Koran*. They do more than reinforce the Arabicity of the Qur'anic text; they also celebrate its mellifluous strokes, its luxuriant colors, and its balanced tones.

In short, these illuminations make of the Qur'an not just a polyphony of sound and meaning but also a visual masterpiece. In that sense the latest edition of *The Message of the Qur'an* has no predecessor. Its sole counterpoint among recent renditions is the graphic *Koran* of Sandow Birk. *American Qur'an* still reflects the text but through a visual, metonymic strategy. It projects the whole in the part, evoking a sense of wonder through the eye, not the ear. Instead of an original translation, the reader finds English translations of particular verses selected to register a moment in American history. I call this the Graphic *Koran*. At once visual and visionary, it is a hybrid genre designed to reach a new audience not previously engaged either by the *Koran* or by Islam. Its instigator and foremost practitioner is the Californian printmaker Sandow Birk. In a dialogic approach to the Word of God, he began his quest by spending a decade in travel and exploration of several sites in Islamic parts of Asia and Africa. He then devoted nine years of his life to creating what he terms "a personal Qur'an." It appeared in print in November 2015 (figure 9).[1]

So bold and multitiered is *American Qur'an* that it needs to be analyzed at three levels:

1. *American Qur'an* may seem to be just another version of the *Koran* in English. A "mere" *transcription* of other English language *Koran*s, it features multiple extant translations even while its creator

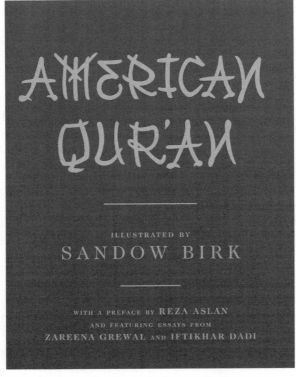

FIGURE 9. Cover of Sandow Birk, *American Qur'an*

delves deeper into the language of these prior efforts in order to forge from them his own pastiche
of the sacred text.

2. And so beyond the text itself, *American Qur'an*
becomes an artistic *adaptation*, complementing
the *Koran*ic text with American scenes, from city
blocks, public spaces, and rural settings, with

special attention to pivotal moments that mark the United States in the early twenty-first century. *American Qur'an* is an adaptation that explores so many new avenues for grasping the Qur'anic message that it becomes not only an adaptation but also a transformation, shifting the lens with which others view, use, and apply Qur'anic themes.

3. At its deepest level, *American Qur'an* is transformed into an ethical lamppost, an *illuminated Koran* that illumines not only the "daily" events but also scenes that stretch and challenge the moral imagination of readers/viewers of its pages. Whether thinking about seasonal catastrophes at home or US military ventures abroad during the past fifteen years, one finds a familiar but discomforting set of pictures. Each mirrors the Qur'anic message in an American context. These cautionary tales are at once vivid and provocative.

In sum, *American Qur'an* combines a transcription, an adaptation, and an illumination into one large, luxuriant book. All three tangents interact to make the book more than another *Koran*; collectively they frame the ancient text as a novel translation, a graphic *Koran*. In the hands of Sandow Birk, and in his own words, the Qur'an becomes "like an onion; the deeper you dig the more you learn, as layer upon layer of meaning unfolds."[2]

American Qur'an: A "Mere" Transcription

In spring 2016 I contacted the artist to clarify the origins and scope of this unusual addition to *Koran*s in English. Birk was as amiable as he was blunt. Humble and direct, he provided in-depth commentary on his approach. "Is not your work a translation?" I asked. "No," he demurred: "it is an adaptation."[3] Of course, he is right. *American Qur'an* is an adaptation, but it is also both less and more than an adaptation. It is at first glance a "mere" transcription, and while it is also an artistic adaptation, it evolves through successive panels into an ethical guidepost, an illumination.

Let us first examine how it is a "mere" transcription. It could be termed a transcription since Sandow Birk has created a sparkling, and also randomized, transcription of the entire text of the Holy Qur'an: 6,236 verses culled and collected in 114 chapters, each with its own illustrated border. But where to begin? I begin where Birk himself begins, with the text. Birk is deft in his use of myriad translations. He himself declares that he "uses copyright-free English translations of the Qur'an from various authors." He does not translate afresh but transposes and copies each verse from a variety of extant translations.

It is difficult to imagine the labor and the dedication required for this project. The inspiration came from the American invasion of Iraq. Birk was working on prints related to the war at its outset, in spring 2003. He wanted to know more about the culture and the religion of those who lived in a region now occupied by American armed forces. He went into a local bookstore to buy his first copy of the Qur'an in translation. It was likely Thomas Cleary, *The Qur'an: A New Translation* (2004). Later he also bought a copy of Muhammad Asad, *The Message of the Qur'an* (1980), as also T. B. Irving, *The Qur'an: The First American Version* (1985). Reading through these several translations, he also went online, to the HUC/USC website, which features three further translations—Yusuf Ali, Marmaduke Pickthall, and M. H. Shakir. In all, Birk estimates, he may have consulted six to eight translations as he pondered how to render the sacred text into a platform of insight for Americans—civilians as well as soldiers—now immersed in first Afghanistan (2001) and then Iraq (2003) as theaters of war.[4]

The one translation most often linked to *American Qur'an* is Rodwell (1861). It was a grudging choice rather than a bracing resource. "The only reason I used Rodwell's translation," explains Birk, "is because it is copyright free. A previous project of mine was based on *The Divine Comedy*, and so I learned that having permission to use a translation is crucial. I probably would have used Cleary mostly, because it seems more concise and clear and simple to me, but I am worried that one of those translators would be upset if I used their translation and could stop my project from being published."

Birk went on to note that he might have contacted Asad or Cleary a decade ago about using their translations, but it was not likely that either scholar or (in Asad's case) his executor would've agreed to this effort "to make an illustrated *Koran*." And so Birk opted for Rodwell but without the archaic pronouns, or awkward phrases or problematic syntax, and also with concern for contemporary viewers/readers of his project. All these decisions attest to Birk's rapt devotion to *American Qur'an*, his unswerving commitment to produce an illustrated—or better, an illuminated—*Koran*.

Specific Translation Choices in *American Qur'an*

Although Rodwell was but one of six to eight translators consulted, and even though he was chosen more for convenience then for engagement with the Qur'anic message, his influence still pervades the transcribed text. The early reliance on Rodwell seems confirmed with the opening *basmala*: In the Name of God the Compassionate, the Merciful. It exactly mirrors Rodwell, but then it veers in multiple, other directions in what follows:

> *In the Name of God the Compassionate, the Merciful*
>   (Rodwell)[5]
> *Praise be to God, Lord of the Universe* (Cleary)
> *Most Gracious, the Most Merciful* (Yusuf Ali)[6]
> *Master of the Day of Judgment* (Pickthall, Yusuf Ali)
> *You alone we worship; You alone we ask for help*
>   (Pickthall)
> *Guide us in the right path* (Palmer, M. H. Shakir)[7]
> *Those whom You have blessed, not of those who have
>   deserved wrath, nor of those who stray* (Abdel
>   Haleem, Yusuf Ali).[8]

In the longer trajectory of this passage, one must scrutinize Birk's choices. The rendition "right path," central to the entire Qur'anic message, is at odds with "straight path," preferred by most translators (Pickthall and Yusuf Ali as well as Asad and Cleary). The most immediate antecedent is M. H. Shakir (1968), which is itself a close paraphrase of Muhammad Ali (1917), though E. H. Palmer (1880) had first broached this option, and indeed Palmer's rendition is closer to Birk's than M. H. Shakir's: "Guide us *in* the right path" versus "Guide us *on* the right path." The choice of preposition is less notable or decisive than the choice of adjective. While "straight" is a geographic metaphor, "right" is an ethical signpost: the right path is the one that involves moral vision and conscious intent, and it is that insistent ethical stance that dominates Birk's entire transcription, at once evoking the original Qur'an and retelling its message in twenty-first-century Americana (figure 10).[9]

Further evidence of how Birk charts his own direction and imparts a distinct tone to his *Koran* transcription appears in Q 36: Ya Sin, reproduced on the cover (figure 11).

Unlike the Opening, which evokes urban America through the Manhattan skyline, this scene is one of some midwestern farmland. Etched with long stretches of brown field, on the right is a distant silo and farmhouse sitting behind green bushes while on the left a modern green tractor/grain harvester trolls and emits smoke, contrasting with the white clouds, occluded, but framing the revealed word that occupies center place in these two plates.

FIGURE 10. Fatiha/Opening from *American Qur'an* (Sandow Birk), with the translation embedded in the Manhattan skyline

The image becomes effective as a border for Q 36 since one of its verses proclaims: "Right before them is the dead earth. We make it produce the grain they eat" (Q 36:33).

While even the most avid reader would be hard-pressed to find Birk's translation resource for this verse,[10] the chapter itself offers ample clues for his antecedents in

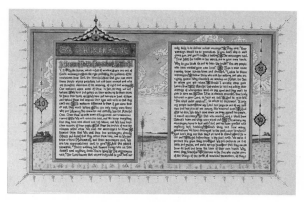

FIGURE 11. Q 36, initial panel from *American Qur'an* (Sandow Birk)

transcribing other verses and also the chapter title. Q 36 is one of several Qur'anic chapters that begins with isolated letters, here Y. S. These letters have puzzled Muslim commentators for centuries and still remain defiant to a consensus interpretation of their meaning. Of major contemporary *Koran* translators, only Muhammad Asad has ventured to make sense of some of these cryptic Arabic letters.[11] For Y. S., Q 36, itself a major liturgical chapter recited at funerals, Birk chooses the title: "O Human Being." Nearly all translators leave Y. S. untranslated. Instead, they give the title as Ya Sin, transliterating the two Arabic letters into English. The title "O Human Being" is not found in Rodwell or Cleary, nor in Yusuf Ali, Pickthall, Shakir, T. B. Irving, Abdel Haleem, or any of the other sources that Birk consulted—save one: Muhammad Asad. It is Asad and Asad alone who translates Ya Sin, rendering it as "O Thou Human Being." Birk, consistent with his practice elsewhere, omits the archaic second person pronoun, and simply transcribes from Asad: "O Human Being," but then in the remainder of the chapter follows Rodwell, though with some interpolations of his own.[12]

Q 36 also offers insight into the relationship between the terms "Qur'an" and "*Koran*," often discussed above. For those readers/viewers of *American Qur'an* who wonder about Birk's shift from the title invocation of Qur'an to the subsequent use of *Koran* in the text, Q 36:2 offers yet another place where Birk is consistent in rendering the Arabic Qur'an as English *Koran*: "By the *Koran*, which is full of wisdom." Rodwell seems to be the antecedent for "*Koran*," here as he is elsewhere throughout *American Qur'an*, but then Birk shifts back to Asad or to Cleary for the phrase "full of wisdom," though he may have gleaned from an online source (Farooq Malik), the dependent clause "which is full of wisdom." Cleary not Asad is likely the immediate choice for verse 1, since Birk begins by citing the initials Y. S., not the phrase "O human being," as does Asad. The full extent of Birk's ability to not just transcribe but also to interpolate the Qur'anic text becomes clear when one considers his rendition of Q 36:1–2 and its likely antecedents:

> *O thou human being! Consider this Qur'an full of wisdom.* (Asad)
> *Ya Sin. By the wise Koran!* (Rodwell)
> *Y.S. By the Recital, full of wisdom.* (Cleary)

Ya Sin. I swear by the Qur'an which is full of wisdom.
   (Farooq Malik)
Y. S. By the Koran, which is full of wisdom. (Birk)

Further Examples of Translation Choices
from *American Qur'an*

The beauty of Birk's high-minded approach to transcribing earlier translations is also evident in his rendition of the final two chapters, known as *al-mu'awwidhatayn*. Each begins by invoking God's protection against evil forces or malicious persons:

Q 113 Daybreak

In the Name of God, the Compassionate, the Merciful.

1 Say, "I take refuge in the Lord of the daybreak
2 from the evil of that which He created,
3 and from the evil of the night when it overtakes me,
4 and from the evil of those who curse,
5 and from the evil of the envious when he envies."

Cleary, Pickthall and Rodwell—all contribute to the above rendition. The tone of what this pastiche accomplishes is much more interesting than its sources. The link to women as sorcerers is frequent for verse 4, reflected in Rodwell's rendition: "weird women," yet Birk follows Cleary's lead in removing any gender association with the verse, instead asking help or rescue from "the evil of those who curse" (whether men or women), even though the final verse, in Cleary as in Pickthall, as in most translators, accents the male actor: "and from the evil of the envious when *he* envies."

It is the same intercalation of Rodwell and Cleary, with some nod to Pickthall, that pervades Birk's rendition of the final chapter:

Q 114 Mankind

In the Name of the Compassion, the Merciful.

1 Say, "I take refuge in the Lord of mankind,
2 the King of mankind,
3 the God of mankind,
4 against the evil of the stealthy whisperer
5 who whispers in the hearts of mankind
6 against djinn and men."

Pickthall/Cleary dominate the first verses while the final three reflect Rodwell with some notable exceptions. "Mankind" in Pickthall/Cleary is clearly preferable to "men" (Rodwell), as is "hearts of mankind" (Cleary) to "men's breasts" (Rodwell).

While there are some flaws in Birk's transcription, they are small and inconsequential.[13] They amount to minor distractions in a capacious canvas, a canvas so capacious that it might do more to lift the *Koran* out of obscurity and into the light of public discourse in twenty-first-century America than any of its precursors. It is the robust nature of its artistry that will occupy us in the remainder of this chapter, as it will all those who venture into the realm of visual exhilaration, at once challenge and hope, that is *American Qurʾan.*

American Qur'an: An Artistic Adaptation

It was not until 2005 that Birk discovered how to link his innate engagement with the *Koran* to his actual performance of the Qur'an as a work of art. Birk had been drawn to the ideal of producing an illustrated *Koran*, with an American audience as his target group, yet he was daunted by the precision of traditional Arabic calligraphy. In residence at the Ballinglen Arts Foundation, he took off a morning to surf in Dublin and then went to the Chester Beatty Library that afternoon. "They had cases and cases of *Koran*s going back 1,000 years," recalls Birk. "They were all hand-painted, and there were all these mistakes, and parts were erased. Suddenly, they went from seeming like this perfect, jeweled thing to something made by a human being. I was like, 'I can do this.'" His goal now seemed attainable: "to depict the banal aspects of daily (American) life in juxtaposition with the divine text."

Birk's deepest commitment to the Qur'an project came from his overriding sense of global citizenry. An artist by trade, he was also a surfer by choice. Traveling the world as an avid surfer had meant that he'd spent extended periods of time in Muslim countries such as Morocco and Indonesia, as well as the Muslim-majority island of Mindanao in the southern Philippines, during the last decade of the twentieth century.

Then came 9/11, and soon after the US invasion of Afghanistan, followed by the invasion of Iraq. Birk saw how Islam was being demonized in the US media.: "I was really following the news every day," he recalls, "just paying attention to the American discourse about 9/11, the war in Iraq and Afghanistan, and listening to all this talk about 'Is Islam fundamentally at odds with the West? Is this a clash of cultures?'"

In order to move beyond the headlines, he had to find new resources. In 2003, after picking up an English-language copy of the Muslim holy text at a Long Beach bookstore, he began researching the *Koran*. "Every day, I learned something new," he says. "The *Koran* is different from the Bible, in that the Bible is basically a narrative from the beginning of the world through the life of Jesus, in sequence. [The *Koran*] is the voice of God speaking directly to you, and it assumes you've already read the Bible and you know the story of Noah and Jesus already."

As he began choosing images to mark each chapter, Birk sought specific passages of the text that he could illustrate in a way that would be relevant to an American audience. What worked best, he acknowledges, were moments when he found something meaningful in the Qur'an that illumines, and almost seems to prefigure, what is happening in twenty-first-century America. He also wanted a broad scope, covering as much of American geography as possible and also finding illustrations to reflect all aspects of American life.

Not surprisingly, there is recurrent reference to his home state and to its topography. Many borders evoke multiple images of Southern California—waterfront, freeways, street scenes showing suburban sprawl and urban blight—but there is also attention to stretches of farmlands, for example, Q 18 "The Cave," folio 2, and also

Q 36, folio 1, to national park picnics (possibly Yellowstone in Q 15 "Rock City"), and oil drilling (likely in Oklahoma; Q 52 "The Mountain"). Familiarity with the scenes does not automatically translate into appreciation for, or connection with, the *Koran*ic text. In each instance, the register of language challenges the reader/viewer to find the connective phrase or verse in the pages transcribed, then framed with Americana. There is no sidebar or appendix providing the link intended and favored by the artist. For some, this will be a daunting challenge, but it is also the challenge that faces all "visitors" to the Qur'an: no one but God knows its deepest meaning, yet all are invited to find "the right path" and so to be guided on that path by these 6,236 verses sorted out into 114 chapters.

Birk likes not only to draw but also to count. Among his self-stated goals is to make reference to each of the fifty states. In one chapter, Q 61 "Battle Line," he portrays a national presidential convention. Before the candidate with his face on the overhead screen surrounded by American flags are banners from several state convention delegates. They number over twenty, some larger (Florida, California, Texas), others smaller (Washington, Nebraska, Alaska). During an election year,[14] the title and the message seem almost interchangeable. Other chapters forge links to the past. They capture a single event that matches a historical moment in that state: Katrina floods for New Orleans (Louisiana), Q 21 "The Prophets," folio 3, opposite a page where one of the references is to Job, losing his family, and the other to Jonah speaking from within the whale, and then the Massey mining accident in West Virginia (April 2010) lining the border of Q 18 "The Cave" folio 1, where the discussion in the Qur'anic text is about the seven sleepers in a cave and their dog. It is never easy or obvious to see how image and text reinforce a single message, but the pause, then reflection make it possible to interface Arabia with America together, neither one occluding the other, instead each echoing or opening a window for the other.

Birk avows that his own religious life is uncomplicated by creedal preferences or institutional alliances. Self-described as "not a man of faith,"[15] he is nonetheless drawn to spiritual themes, beginning with the American Qur'an project itself. There are scenes of immigrant women in Q 19 "Mary," and also in several others. Some of the most compelling scenes stretch over several panels. One of the most compelling and intricate is Q 4 "Women," an oft-cited chapter with provocative themes/ verses, an eight-page spread involving a cycle-of-life story, each marked by the American flag. The first unfolds on the steps of a US government federal building, among them a returning coffin, then a wedding, followed by detectives investigating a nighttime murder scene. Then comes a burial, but even the dead continue to influence this world, as a group of teenage skateboarders use the spot of the burial to practice their ollie skills.

Similarly, in illustrating one sura (Q 24 Light) that calls for women to cover their heads, Birk wondered out loud whether non-Muslim American women typically do the same. He came up with the idea for a panel showing a woman whose head and face are protected by a heavy hat and scarf, walking next to her another woman also covered and wearing glasses, both of them braving the fierce wind of a Chicago snowstorm.[16] For those who first see this image, then read the matching Qur'anic verse, the connection may seem remote. Does the panel really translate from Muslim to non-Muslim women? These two sets of women may actually seem to have nothing to do with each other, and here is but one of many instances where the reader/viewer could come to a different conclusion than the artist: perhaps the women in a Chicago snowstorm do not translate into the women from seventh-century Arabia or modern-day Saudi Arabia. That rejection of a correspondence, however, provides yet another way that *American Qur'an* resembles the original Qur'an, challenging its listeners/readers to rethink who they are and what they most value.

Throughout the *Koran*, Birk noticed how the text repeatedly reminds the reader that the words are coming directly from heaven. "So a lot of my pictures," he observes, "are about messages coming down from the sky: satellites in outer space, newspaper-distribution centers, television talk shows, guys fixing telephone lines, a guy putting up a satellite dish on his roof. All these are different ways we are sending messages around."[17] Again, the metaphysical resonance of modern-day communications may not seem evident, or convincing, to skeptics, yet Birk is intent to make all viewers/readers think or rethink the axial points of their worldview.

American Qur'an: An Illuminated *Koran*, with Ethical Urgency

More than descriptive insight into American daily life, connection to women's dress codes across time, or reference to communications specific to the twenty-first century, *American Qur'an* is also an ethical commentary on the United States, on both America and Americans abroad as well as at home. The key to his moral message is metaphor.

Nine years after he had begun his work, in July 2014, Birk finally completed *American Qur'an*. He had not just transcribed the entire sacred text but also had produced 230 illuminated, table-sized pages of the *Koran*. "My pictures are not of what the text is saying," explains Birk, "but a metaphor for what the text is saying."

And so the cumulative force of these visual metaphors offers insight into Birk's avowedly personal, yet fully scriptural, approach to his own role as a citizen artist. While all artists communicate and most are devoted to the message they impart, what sets Birk apart is his sense of how the artist must be a responsible, and reflective, citizen. He honors the past while connecting to the present at the same time as he imagines a future of engagement without rancor, truth without orthodoxy, submission without punishment.

"Following the traditions of ancient Arabic and Islamic manuscripts," notes his website, "Birk hand-transcribed the entire English-translated text of the Qur'an as was done in centuries past. . . . Adapting the techniques and stylistic devices of Arabic and Persian painting and albums, Birk blends the past with the present, the East with the West, creating an 'American Qur'an'."[18]

These techniques are put in the service of his personal vision as a printmaker. Neither a theologian nor a scholar of Islam, he is a professional artist focused on the word as hallowed hope. His calling often seems more monastic than iconoclastic. He declared, in a recent interview: "The idea of making a whole book all by yourself like a monk used to do in the Middle Ages, that was interesting to me as an artist because it's something people don't do nowadays."[19] Notes his principal gallerist, Catharine Clark, "Sandow felt compelled to approach the aesthetics of his version of the Qur'an as if each *sura* were a page in a medieval devotional Book of Hours, or an illuminated holy manuscript."[20] And so in *American Qur'an*, Birk scrupulously follows traditional guidelines: ink colors, page formatting and headings, margin sizes, down to the medallions marking verses and passages—all recall and recreate, insofar as possible, patterns with Islamic precedents. What is boldly American is his hand-lettered calligraphy. It relies on a contemporary American tradition of writing: the street letters of urban graffiti that Birk observed in his native Los Angeles neighborhood.

Even more boldly American are the images. Once he transcribed each page, he illuminated one central theme with scenes from contemporary American life. Examples abound. Many have already been noted: they range from labor to politics to leisure. Still others command our attention. Q 18 "The Cave" elides men in the cave with West Virginia miners. Q 54 "The Moon" suggests space exploration directed to a lunar landing, while Q 61 "The Battle Line" connects the battle line to electoral politics at a presidential convention. Much later, Q 108 "The Chargers" features race cars, whether at the Daytona Five Hundred or some other site. Q 113 "Dawn" finds surfers in the early morning on the California coast.

For those puzzled by this hybrid genre, its closest precedent equivalent is the graphic novel. A comic book featuring adult themes, the graphic novel draws the reader into a single image but the image then immediately forces you back into the text. You cannot understand either without an intensive cross reading, an engaged, multiple sighting, of both picture and word. In one sense, Birk is using transgressive art to advance progressive politics. Here are uncomfortable scenes of America at home and abroad: the militarized US-Mexico border, the Guantanamo prison camp in Cuba, and landscapes devastated by war in Japan and Iraq. At the same time, there are scenes of everyday life: women during childbirth, garbage collectors passing morning strollers, supermarkets teeming with varied customers. All are welded together in a sumptuous format, each element— the title, the page, the painting around the borders, the script(ure) in a text box—invites puzzlement. It is as though each feature elides with and requires the other to be understood, even fleetingly. While no final judgment is possible, curiosity is sparked, insight enabled, into what could be, and here becomes, an American Qur'an. The ethical dimension may seem mute, yet it lurks just beneath the surface in almost every instance.

It is crucial to think not just of the book printed but the book exhibited. In an exhibition format, even more than in a printed book, the moral message projects. Part of the genius of this unprecedented work is the bridge it affords from gallery site to book form, and that bridge offers a bold ethical mandate. *American Qur'an* began as a traveling exhibition before it became a printed book. The book took shape through successive exhibitions,[21] and the challenge of mounting an exhibit of so many panels led Birk to make a further decision: to create a directional sign, a way of focusing the viewer/reader on the ethical content of what s/he is seeing. Just as Birk matched moments from American daily life and recent history with Qur'anic chapters, so he matched the physical space for his exhibitions with an everyday American fixture: the ATM machine.

An ATM machine?! In an economy run by efficiency, and riveted to instant access, the ATM is as common as it is neglected in the catalog of twenty-first-century Americana. It is important to recall that the Ka'ba, before it became the orientation focus for the new Muslim movement, was itself a storehouse of profane idols. As I noted in chapter two, the Holy House became a place that Abraham shared with others, with idols that represented local gods and tribal deities. Similarly, Birk has elected to transform the idolatrous ATM frame into the mosque interior element known as a *mihrab*. The *mihrab* is a niche found in the wall of every mosque: it indicates the *qibla*, or direction, marking the Black Stone (Ka'ba) in Mecca, toward which Muslims face when praying. The ATM machine as *qibla* is, of course, ironic. It highlights Birk's insistence on the need to rethink values and moral choices as a daily practice, to monitor constantly, and unflinchingly, who we are against the highest ideals of who we should be. Idols are not just objects, they are also instincts and behaviors. In Birk's hand, or rather his hand supplemented by the hands of his wife, who is a ceramicist, the ATM shape becomes a *qibla* epitomizing and channeling the message of the entire Qur'an (figures 12 and 13), and so Islam: to strive for the best that we can humanly be.

To date, there have been four American *mihrab*s created, and while each reflects Birk's distinctive ethos, the first, in white background with blue letters, depicted in figures 12 and 13, projects his intent: to offer evocative phrases from the Qur'an that summarize its message but also goad the viewer/reader to think about its daily, moral application. As noted earlier, al-Jurjānī, an eleventh-century literary critic, observed that the marvel of the Qur'an, its *i'jaz*, or inimitability, was best understood through the verse, not the chapter, as the crucial unit of analysis.[22] And so the four verses selected for this, the first American *mihrab*, are decisive:

Always be just (top)—Q 5:18
Be true to every promise (right)—Q 17:34
Truly with hardship comes ease (bottom)—Q 94:5–56
Be modest in your bearing (left)—Q 31:19

FIGURE 12. Sandow Birk, *American Mihrab*

Each of these verses reflects the artist's penchant for meditating on the verses as he transcribes them, then clarifying what are the central ethical guidelines to retrieve from the Noble Book. It is crucial to note once again the subtle but persistent influence of Asad. The two works—*The Message of the Qur'an* and *American Qur'an*—seem to project a stark contrast. After all, *American Qur'an*

FIGURE 13. Sandow Birk standing in front at right side of same plate

provides no Arabic text or even reference to al-Qur'an in Arabic, and yet Birk relies heavily on Asad's translation for his own transcriptions. He also provides a unique commentary on Asad's pointillist insights in the above citations. All take their wording in English from *The Message of the Qur'an*; all are stronger in Asad's version than in parallel renditions. Their collective import as a *qibla*, not only for viewers but also for the artist himself, is underscored by figure 13: the author standing in front of the first American *mihrab*, as if to signal his own allegiance to the words/the apodictic aphorisms that he has etched for his exhibit of *American Qur'an*.

The same ethical insistence characterizes other scenes in panels from *American Qur'an*. As noted above, Birk includes not only "daily" events and scenes from immigrant, urban life but also scenes that challenge American military ventures of the twenty-first century. At once moral accents and ethical mandates, they compel each visitor to rethink what is the import of warfare, from seventh-century Arabia to twenty-first-century America. The scenes are especially graphic in two chapters: Q 8 "Spoils of War" and Q 105 "The Elephant." The first comes near the beginning of *American Qur'an*. It contains three plates. The first sketches a gasoline station under a sign advertising "MOBIL," its red, white, and blue colors paralleling but also parodying American patriotic colors. The second shows American troops patrolling in Afghanistan, clearly the site of conflict because of the terrain but also the Persian/Arabic letters fragmentary yet revealing "Afgha(nistan)." The third portrays figures being guarded in a prison camp, hunched over or kneeling in bright orange suits and goggles, sharply contrasting with the upright brown-clad soldiers who surround them. A sign in the background reads: Camp X Ray-Guantanamo. Profits-patrols-prisoners, all three relate to the Arab wars of the early seventh century, taken as historical precursor and eerie parallel to American wars in the early twenty-first century.

Sometimes the reader/viewer will struggle with the import of the visual/literary message conveyed by the *Koran* chapter juxtaposed with a troubling image. In the third plate from Q 8 "The Spoils," for instance, the image of prisoners at Guantanamo seems to reflect the verse: "It is not fit for a prophet to have captives until he has subdued the land" (Q 8:67). Once again, the antecedent translator is Cleary (not Rodwell or Asad), and since Cleary, like Birk, offers the passage without commentary, the uninitiated must seek some commentary from other sources. It is a revelation given to the Prophet Muhammad at the time of his battle with the Quraish, toward the end of his life, and the double implication is: (1) the war must be just, and (2) the captives must be freed once the war is over (Q 47:4). Read in this context, the captives at Camp X Ray occupy an ambivalent status: Were the US wars in Afghanistan and Iraq "just"? If so, once they have been concluded (with the withdrawal of US troops in direct combat), then must not the captives be freed?

That same query/message, restated in Q 47 "Muhammad," is etched by Birk's panels surrounding the text:

here we find the combatants at risk, with two panels showing an American patrol under attack in Iraq, attending to a casualty from their own ranks. The relevant message, however, seems to come from Q 47:35: "Don't be fainthearted then, and slacken towards peace, you are bound to rise high in the end. God is with you and will never let your good deeds go to waste." This translation, combined from Rodwell and Asad, underscores the moral imperative of war: if it is just, then the bloodshed, like the taking of captives, will not be in vain. Still, the central query pervades, in seventh-century Arabia as in twenty-first-century America: was the cause of war—*casus belli*, literally, case for war—just in the case of the Iraq war? Although no definitive answer has been given, Birk allows one to reflect on the larger frame within which all war is waged.

A similar moral message about war and warfare is coded in a single panel found on the border of Q 105. Toward the end, *Koran*ic chapters are very short, so short that both Q 105 "The Elephant" and Q 106 "The Quraish" are paired on the same page. Yet the panel evokes the background to "The Elephant." Its motif predates the rise of Islam, when pagan Mecca was being invaded by Ethiopian/Yemeni forces from the south. Their intent was to destroy the Ka'ba, or Black Stone, in Mecca, but they were thwarted by flying creatures—birds or insects— who attacked the invaders and spared the Meccans' occupation, as well as likely destruction of their major sanctuary. Birk has captured the scene with a dusty brown terrain. It features a tank with seven binocular-armed soldiers moving on patrol, while outside them, and outside the panel border, flutter seventeen birds all in flight, some gazing at, others away, from the scene that unfolds next to them.

Besides demonstrating Birk's penchant to link America and Arabia, the seventh to the twenty-first century, the Q 105 panel underscores not just his careful transcription of the *Koran* in English but also his attention to commentaries on the text. Just as there is no explanation for "just war" in the texts of Q 8 or Q 47, so nothing in the revealed Qur'an tells the reader who were "the troops with the elephants" and how they were foiled by "flocks of birds, pelting them with rock-hard clay." All these phrases come from Cleary's translation, used here by Birk, but as we have seen above, Birk often consults Rodwell and Asad as well as Cleary. In this case it is likely that he relies on *The Message of the Qur'an*: powerfully on display for aphoristic dicta displayed in the American *mihrab*, Asad's rendition also offers extended commentary that supports, even as it amplifies, the bold depiction of watchful birds of prey in the panel for Q 105.

There are numerous other passages that provide a reminder of the dangers of military action, for those who invade and hope to conquer, as for those who are the intended victims, or beneficiaries, of conquest. Far from a one-sided message of resistance and pacifism, these panels call each citizen to weigh carefully what is intended, and what results, from warfare, whether initiated in Arabia or America, in the seventh or the twenty-first century.[23]

Birk and Rodwell

No conclusion on the saga of the *Koran* in English can ignore the novelty and the challenge of Birk's *American Qur'an*. Birk's bold initiative to make a personal Qur'an evokes wonder, but it also compels judgment, from non-Muslim readers. Those who hate Muslims and revile the *Koran* will not be won over by *American Qur'an*. Others, however, will benefit from its "onion peels"—at once visceral and visible. They will be compelled to follow Birk's self-examination. In the aftermath of 9/11, they, like he, have been asking, and must keep asking: Who are Muslims? What is their Holy Book? Does Islam have a consistent message? And what about me? How does the Qur'anic message apply to me, whether I am Muslim or not, in my everyday life, as I wrestle with scenes of Muslim life that involve American soldiers as well as Arab terrorists, in places overseas but also at home?

In keeping with the goal of my own book, I would argue that Birk's translation choices—a pastiche with subjective, sensitive, and consistently superlative choices—are as critical as the images he creates to border them. Actually, his images exceed their borders. They are more like the medieval Book of Hours. They have much more heft than a border in visually communicating the content of the text. They provoke each reader/viewer to consider the semiotics of images in relation to the sacred text. What is sacred is juxtaposed with the seemingly profane and colloquial, only to have its sacredness bolstered rather than tarnished.

Even Birk's choice of Rodwell exceeds the limits of his motive for its selection. I would argue that he fulfills the mandate laid down by Peachy and cited above, to wit, that "the English text must stand on its own merits, apart from not next to the original Arabic." Birk's initial goal may have been pragmatic—to avoid copyright challenges—but in choosing to follow Rodwell, even with adumbrations and admixtures from other translations, and even though he may have decided in the end that he did not like Rodwell, Birk is still "employing a form of English with a classical sound that befits august scripture."

That commendation of Rodwell comes not from Birk but from a twenty-first-century moral philosopher, Robert Wright. Wright, like Birk, is a seasoned professional operating outside the guild of Islamic studies and beyond the screen of Muslim orthodoxy. Wright has authored a sweeping book on Abrahamic faith, *The Evolution of God*.[1] Wright's goal is to defend religion as itself a pillar of society. In his view, religion reinforces and expands social order, along with, not against, the dictates of science. Wright appeals to the natural argument—how the universe itself reflects a "divine" pattern. Wright

CONCLUSION

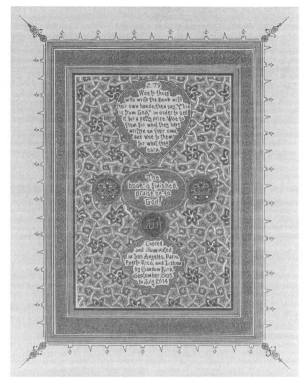

FIGURE 14. Colophon for Sandow Birk, *American Qur'an*

finds in the *Koran* a rich source to mine. But how to mine it? Since Wright, like Birk, cannot read Arabic, he must mine the *Koran*ic message in English. Wright's preferred translator? Rodwell, and he would nod in recognition at the final page of Birk's almost decade-long endeavor (figure 14).

The devout closure in this colophon commingles the accent of Rodwell with the language of Cleary. It does so with the same deft subtlety that marks all the verses and chapters that precede it. In a page reminiscent of medieval illuminated manuscripts, minus human images, Birk gives praise to God (also with Allah written in Arabic: ﷲ). He cites the exact months/years of his endeavor: September 2005 to July 2014. It is a work of devotion, etched in humility and offered with hope that its reception will justify the artist's prolonged labor.

Future Prospect of *American Qur'an*

Despite its unprecedented boldness and intense moral energy, as well as the doggedness, creativity, and good will of its initiator, the fate of *American Qur'an* is indeterminate. In an early review, from 2010, art critic Holland Cotter noted: "Even in English, the *Koran* is rhetorically powerful in a way that Mr. Birk's illustrations are not," but he quickly qualifies that sweeping judgment: "whatever the final strengths and weaknesses of his work," adds Cotter, "Birk is paying close, complicated attention to what may be *the single most important, and least understood, book in the world at present*. Just by trying to introduce it to a new audience, and to do so with maximum ease and minimum harm, *American Qur'an* is an ambitious and valuable undertaking."[2]

One cannot predict what will be the long-term reception of *American Qur'an*. It both clarifies and complicates the import of *Koran*ic dicta. Does one focus on the Twin Towers burning as the backdrop of Q 44 "The Smoke," or the dramatic space craft in orbit that frames Q 54 "The Moon"? Both fit the twin texts: an Arabic now English *Koran* bracketed with modern Americana. Perhaps one needs to ponder both, acknowledging the expansive spirit of openness that marks, and indeed exceptionalizes, Birk's venture into the sea storm of translation. "By mixing and matching translations to arrive at his version," declares Willow Wilson, "Birk has inadvertently created one of the most accessible interpretations of the *Koran* in English, but also one of the most ideologically opaque. This is neither the literalist translation propagated by the Saudis nor the rationalist one composed by Muhammad Asad, nor the stilted interpretation popularized by the Victorians (such as Sales and, later, Arberry). It is something else, something more comforting but less instructive. This, too, is profoundly American."[3] One can dare to hope that *American Qur'an* signals not the end but the next phase, a new beginning, for the *Koran* in English. It is, after all, "the single most important, and least understood, book in the world at present," and no other scholar or artist has tried so boldly to make its message relevant to our times and our challenges.

A Workable Marriage?

In looking back over nearly 900 years—from Robert of Ketton in 1134 to Georges Sale in 1734 to Yusuf Ali and

Marmaduke Pickthall in the 1930s to A. J. Arberry in 1955 to Muhammad Asad in 1980 to Thomas Cleary in 2004 and now Sandow Birk in 2016—one is reminded of the image of an awkward, ageless couple. They come from different backgrounds. Barely acquainted, they pursue a lengthy courtship. It extends over centuries. The wary bride is quite beautiful, alluring, yet resistant to all suitors: she wants to stay faithful to her family. The foreign groom, equally reluctant to marry anyone outside his own insular family, finds the prospective bride irresistible. He persists. She, after much hesitation, agrees to wed this dauntless stranger. They become an odd but stable couple.

The woman is the Qur'an, the suitor, English. The wife alas must change her name. The Arabic Qur'an becomes first the Latin and then the English *Koran*. Some flirtatious onlookers play with both. Earlier we saw how the name of Pickthall's translation shifted from *The Meaning of the Glorious Koran* to *The Meaning of the Glorious Qur'an*. Birk's *American Qur'an* also announces a compromise in the title, yet in all that follows it invokes only the *Koran*.[4] Several translators insist on using just the Qur'an. Despite compromises and tensions, the Arabic Qur'an/the English *Koran* endures, projecting a strained yet workable marriage. Its offspring now occupy not just North America and the United Kingdom but also disparate parts of Asia; Turks and Pakistanis, Indians and Malays share interest in, and devotion to, the English *Koran* as well as the Arabic Qur'an. While the virtual world of the twenty-first century may not have produced a marriage made in heaven, it is one that can, and will continue to, function on earth. An Arabic Qur'an has become the English *Koran*.

Although neither party surrenders elements of memory, outlook, and hope that exceed the bonds of marriage, within its confines new vistas and new partnerships have become possible. Nowhere is this compromise more evident, or more promising, than in *American Qur'an*. "*Koran* (throughout) is the current name," acknowledges Birk, "yet Qur'an (in the title) is respectful of Islamic history and Muslim preference."[5] Scanning its pages, where visual insight meshes with literary signs, where past and future blend in the present, we find traces of Arabic as the *Koran* struggles to be, and to remain, clear in its message for all generations, for all places, and for all peoples.

Just as the colophon signals the completion of Birk's decade-long labor, so it also marks the nimble embrace of two linguistic, cultural, and religious registers that Birk constantly pursues, as do all *Koran* translators. For those who arrive at the end of *American Qur'an*, "Praise be to God!" on the final page translates the Arabic phrase, *Al-hamdulillah*. Its last word is literally Allah, since *lillah* means "to Allah" or "to God." Both names—Allah and God—are correct. Both are widely used. Each is linked to the linguistic register of its user.

Allah in al-Qur'an becomes God in the *Koran*, yet the latter continues to mirror the former. Neither displaces the other. Each retains its value and benefit. Those who read and recite the *Koran*, whether Muslim or non-Muslim, offer praise to God but also, echoing al-Qur'an, to Allah/الله. The Name, together with the Book, retain their primacy in Arabic without losing their value in English. To paraphrase Ibrahim Abu Nab, "they cannot be translated but they must be translated." *Al-hamdulillah*, Praise be to God!

ACKNOWLEDGMENTS

Many are the individuals—family, friends, colleagues, mentors, and editors—who have made possible the completion of this book, gestating for more than fifty years and in the making for more than five.

I am indebted to Fred Appel, with whom I had worked on an earlier Princeton book project, for inviting me to participate in this series on Lives of Great Religious Books. A decade ago, I had written a book on *The Qur'an: A Biography* (Atlantic Books, 2006). Fred spurred me to think about a sequel that concerned solely the Noble Book, as the Qur'an is often known, in English translation. I accepted the challenge, only to find that I needed many hands, ears, and eyes as well as nimble minds to complete the task. Others from Princeton University Press—Thalia Leaf, Debbie Tegarden, and Dawn Hall—facilitated the manuscript at crucial stages in its preparation and production.

Among family, my daughters Rachel and Anna have read parts of the book and provided valuable feedback. My wife, miriam cooke, has read the entire manuscript, more than once, always attentive to literary issues that sometimes have eluded or befuddled me. She also arranged for a group of colleagues—Omid Safi, Erdag

Goknar, Kristine Stiles, and Kathy O'Dell—to come to our home and have a dinner conversation devoted mostly to chapter seven, "The Graphic *Koran*"; the chapter examines the brilliant creation of Sandow Birk, *American Qur'an* (Liveright, 2015). I am indebted to all of them for crystalline insight and productive suggestions. Other colleagues, further afield, provided resources from their own research that enabled and expanded my own reflections: Volker Greifenhagen for a gemlike essay on Qur'an translation, Brett Wilson for analyses of early twentieth-century translators, and especially Shawkat Toorawa for lyrical renditions that evoke for English readers the aesthetic appeal of al-Qur'an in Arabic.

Images are integral to seeing, not just reading, the *Koran* in English. I had superb support from Duke University art history specialists, John Taormina and Jack Edinger, and from Duke Library collection specialists, Sean Swanick and Lee Sorensen. They helped me first locate, then reproduce the figures that are crucial to this book, but above all, I am indebted to Sandow Birk and to the Catharine Clark Gallery for providing me multiple images of *American Qur'an* for chapter seven, as also the central image from sura Ya Sin (Q 36) for the jacket cover.

I am also grateful for the sparkling friendship of two lifelong associates, both scholars of the Qur'an who stimulated my own efforts to make sense of the Noble Book. One is Carl W. Ernst, a colleague at the University of North Carolina–Chapel Hill, with whom I coedit a series on Islamic Civilization and Muslim Networks at the University of North Carolina Press. Carl has written an elegant book, *How to Read the Qur'an* (2011), from which I have benefited, as I have also from a parallel book penned by another good friend, Ziauddin Sardar, *Reading the Qur'an* (2011).

In the largest arc of indebtedness two other individuals stand out. Ibrahim Abu Nab (d. 1991) was a Jordanian scholar of American literature. He hosted me in his Amman home back in the mid-1980s and inspired me to think deeply about the intricacy but also the necessity of rendering the Arabic Qur'an into the *Koran* in English. I dedicated *The Qur'an: A Biography* to Ibrahim. James Kritzeck (d. 1986) was an even earlier, and more decisive, influence on me. In 1958 I stumbled into Kritzeck's seminar on Islamic philosophy, and have been striving to regain my balance ever since. James Kritzeck was my first teacher in Islamic thought and also a subtle translator of *Koran*ic complexities. It is to him that I dedicate this book, a small repayment for a very large debt.

The *Koran* in English by Author and Date

All translations are listed alphabetically, by century and, unless otherwise indicated, without the Arabic text. Also, for further consultation, several entries include websites and other information.

PRE-TWENTIETH CENTURY (THE MOST OFTEN CITED, WITH ONLY 3, 5, 6, AND 7 IN ENGLISH)

1. Robert of Ketton, *Lex Mahumet pseudorprophete que arabice Alcoran—The Religion of Muhammad the Pseudo-Prophet and the Arabic Koran*, Latin (1143).

2. Luther, Martin, *Verlegung des Alcoran*—translation and abridgement of Riccoldo da Monte di Croce, *Contra legem Sarracenorum* ca. 1300, German (1542).

3. Ross, Alexander, *The Alcoran of Mahomet*—trans. from French of Du Ryer (1649).

4. Marracci, Ludovico, *Alcorani textus universus*—ed. and trans. from Arabic into Latin, 2 vols. (1698).

5. Sale, George, *The Koran, Commonly Called the Alcoran of Mohamed. Translated into English from the original Arabic, with explanatory notes, to which is prefixed a preliminary discourse* (1734).

6. Rodwell, J. M., *The Koran*—Everyman's Library, Philosophy and Theology 380 (1861/1909).
7. Palmer, E. H., *The Qur'ān, Translated*—Sacred Books of the East Series, ed. F. Max Muller. Vols. 6 and 9 (1880–82).

TWENTIETH CENTURY

1. Abul Fazl, Mirza, *The Qur'an* (1910).
2. Ahmad, Mirza Bashiruddin Mahmud, *The English Commentary of the Holy Qur'an* (1947–63).
3. Ahmed, Mohamed J., and Samira Ahmed, *The Koran, Complete Dictionary and Literal Translation* (1994). Also available at http://www.clay.smith.name/Lexical _Quran.htm (accessed on October 9, 2016).
4. Ali, Abdullah Yusuf, *The Holy Qur'an: Text, Translation, and Commentary* (1934, multiple editions), including later ones with Arabic text, then reprinted without commentary, and with changes to the title (*The Meaning of the Holy Qur'an*, 1977), and also with de-translation of God to Allah (*The Meaning of the Holy Qur'an*, 1989).
5. Ali, Ahmed, *Al-Qur'an: A Contemporary Translation* (1988), bilingual with facing-page presentation.
6. Ali, Hashim Amir, *The Message of the Qur'an: Presented in Perspective* (1974).
7. Ali, Maulvi Sher, and Mirza Ghulam Ahmad, *The Holy Qur'an—Arabic Text and English Translation* (1936/1955) and then *The Holy Qur'an: English Translation and Short Commentary*, published in 1969. The translation itself is Sher Ali's. After Sher Ali died, Farid completed the commentary that he, Sher, and Mirza Bashir-uddin Mahmud Ahmad had started together. The resulting three-volume-long commentary was

completed in 1963, followed by a single-volume commentary in 1969.

8. Ali, Maulana Muhammad, *The Holy Qur'an: Arabic Text, English Translation, and Commentary* (1917, 4th rev. ed. 1951).

9. Ali, Syed V. Mir Ahmed, and Ayatullah Aqa Mahdi Puya Yazdi (Agha Pooya), *The Holy Qur'an* (1964) (one of multiple Qur'an translations distributed by Tahrike Tarsile Qur'an).

10. Aneesuddin, Mir, *A Simple Translation of the Holy Qur'an* (1993).

11. Arafat, Q., *The Qur'an: The Conclusive Word of God* (1991).

12. Arberry, A. J., *The Koran Interpreted* (1955).

13. Asad, Muhammad, *The Message of the Qur'an* (1980/2003), with Arabic text.

14. Auolakh, Abdul Majeed, *The Holy Qur'an* (1990s).

15. Barelvi, Ahmad Raza Khan, *The Holy Qur'an: An English Translation from Kanzul Iman* (1910/1988) (three separate editions: Hanif Akhtar Fatmi [n.d.], Faridul Haq [1988], Aqib Farid Qadri [2003]), available online at http://www.alahazrat.net/alquran/Quran/ (accessed on October 9, 2016).

16. Behbudi, Muhammad Baqir, with Colin Turner, *The Qur'an: A New Interpretation* (1997).

17. Bell, Richard, *The Qur'an: Translated, with a Critical Rearrangement of the Surahs* (1937–39).

18. Bewley, Abdalhaqq, and Aisha Bewley, *The Noble Qur'an: A New Rendering of Its Meaning in English* (1999). Authorized and requested by Sufi master Darqawi Shadhili Qadiri Shaykh 'Abd al-Qadir al-Sufi (formerly Ian Dallas).

19. Daryabadi, Abdul Majid, *The Glorious Qur'an: Text, Translation, and Commentary* (ca. 1985). An abridged version of his *Tafsir al-Qur'an*, 4 vols. (1981–85), it was originally published as *The Holy Qur'an: With English Translation and Commentary* (1941–57).

20. Dawood, N. J., *The Koran* (1956/1972/1990), at first in a different sura numbering from the traditional arrangement, but then in 1990 edition conforming to the traditional arrangement.

21. Dihlawi, Hairat, *The Qur'an* (1916/1930).

22. Durkee, Abdullah Nooruddeen, and Hajjah Noura Durkee, *The Tajwidi Qur'an*; 1992 (partial); 1999/2003 (complete). Arabic, transliterated, and English. Online at http://www.Koranusa.org/noorudeendurkee.htm.

23. Fakhry, Majid, *The Qur'an—A Modern English Version* (1997).

24. Farid, Malik Ghulam, *The Holy Qur'an with English Translation and Short Commentary* (1969).

25. Al-Ghali, Muhammad Mahmoud, *Towards Understanding the Ever-Glorious Qur'an* (1997).

26. Al Haneef, Iman Torres, *The Holy Qur'an in Plain English* (1993).

27. Hasan, Mahmoodul, and Shabbir Ahmad Usmani, *The Noble Qur'an: Tafseer-e Usmani* (1991).

28. Al-Hayek, 'Izzuddin, *An Approximate, Plain, Straightforward Translation of the Meanings of the Honorable Qur'an in English* (1996).

29. Irving, T. B. (Al Hajj Ta'lim Abu Nasr), *The Qur'an: The First American Version* (1985).

30. Jullundri, Ali Ahmad Khan, *Translation of the Glorious Holy Qur'an, with Commentary* (1962/1978).

31. Khalifa, Rashad, *Qur'an: The Final Testament* (1981/1992).

32. Khan, Muhammad Abdul Hakim, *The Holy Qur'an* (1905).

33. Khan, Muhammad Muhsin, and Muhammad Taqi ud-din al-Hilali, *Interpretation of the Meanings of the Noble Qur'an* (1977/1999), multiple editions, always with Arabic text. (Highly controversial, yet the most widely distributed Qur'an during the past quarter of a century.)

34. Khan, Muhammad Zafrullah, *The Qur'an: Arabic Text and English* (1970).

35. Khatib, Mohammad M., *The Bounteous Koran: A Translation of Meaning and Commentary* (1986).

36. Latif, Syed Abdul, *al-Qur'an* (1969).

37. Malik, Muhammad Farooq-i Azam, *Al-Qur'an, Guidance for Mankind* (1997).

38. Maududi, Syed Abul A'la, *The Meaning of the Qur'an* (1967–88), translated from the Urdu by Muhammad Akbar.

39. Mufassir, Muhammad Ahmad, *The Koran: The First Tafsir in English* (1979).

40. Munshey, Munir, *The Entire Noble Qur'an* (n.d.), available online at http://www.answering-christianity.com /cgi-bin/quran/quran_search.cgi?search_text=&search _type=The+Entire+Noble+Quran&munir_munshey =1&B1=Search (accessed on October 9, 2016).

41. *Al-Muntakhab*. Only available online, it is a collective endeavor to provide an English rendition based on the *tafsir* (commentary), *al-Muntakhab fi tafsir al-Qur'an al-karim* (1978), itself an effort by Egyptian scholars to make the Arabic Qur'an more accessible in translation by rendering each of its verses into contemporary modern Arabic (ca. 1980).

42. Nahaboo, Houssein, *The Holy Qur'an* (1987).

43. Nikayin, Fazlollah, *The Qur'an: A Poetic Translation from the Original* (1999).

44. Nuri, Khadim Rahmani, *The Running Commentary of the Holy Qur'an with Under-Bracket Comments* (1964).

45. Omar, Amatul Rahman, and Abdul Manan Omar, *The Holy Qur'an* (1991).

46. Ozek, Ali, N. Uzunoglu, R. Topuzoglu, and M. Maksutoglu, *The Holy Qur'an with English Translation* (1992). Largely derived, without acknowledgment, from Pickthall 1930 and Yusuf Ali 1937.

47. Parekh, Abdul Ghaffur, *Easy Dictionary of the Qur'an* (3rd ed., 2000). A word-by-word translation of the Qur'an into English.

48. Pathan, M.A.K., *The Meaning of the Qur'an* (1983).

49. Pervez, Ghulam Ahmed, *Exposition of the Holy Qur'an* (1996), an English rendering of the 1961 Urdu translation, *Mafhum-al-Qur'an*.

50. Pickthall, Marmaduke, *The Meaning of the Glorious Koran: An Explanatory Translation* (1930, with multiple subsequent editions, and then revised by El-ʿAshi 1996), with a further revision by Jane A. McAuliffe (2017), all without Arabic text (multiple editions).

51. Ruhi, Firozuddin, *The Qur'an* (1965).

52. Saheeh International, *The Qur'an: English Meanings and Notes* (1997/2004), a translation by three women converts, Amatullah J. Bantley, Umm Muhammad, and Aminah Assami, available online at http://www.islamwb.com/books/Quran-Saheeh-International-English-Translation.pdf (accessed on October 9, 2016) and also in http://www.islamawakened.com under Umm Muhammad (Saheeh International).

53. Salahuddin, Pir, *The Wonderful Koran* (1960).

54. Sarwar, Ghulam, *The Holy Qur'an* (1920).

55. Sarwar, Shaykh Muhammad, *The Holy Qur'an* (1982).

56. Shakir, Mohammedali Habib, *The Qur'an* (1968/1999), without Arabic text (a forgery, reproducing Maulana Mohammed Ali [1917] almost word for word). On this plagiarism, see http://ahmadiyya.org/movement/shakir.htm (accessed on October 9, 2016).

57. Tariq, Abdur Rahman, and Ziauddin Ahmad Gilani, *The Holy Qur'an Rendered into English* (1966).

58. Zayid, Mahmud Yusuf, *The Qur'an: An English Translation of the Meaning of the Qur'an* (1980).

59. Zidan, Ahmad, and Dina Zidan, *The Glorious Qur'an* (1993). Consistently imitating, without acknowledgment, Yusuf Ali (1937).

60. Az-Zindani, Abdul-Majeed, *Holy Qur'an: English Translation of the Meanings and Commentary*, 1985. (Yet another translation directly derived from Yusuf Ali [1937].)

NOTABLE BUT PARTIAL TRANSLATIONS

1. Abdul Karim, Shaikh, *Dawatul Qur'an, Arabic Text, Translation, and Commentary*, (1991–94) in 3 volumes. Author died after only completing eight of thirty parts.

2. Abu Nab, Ibrahim, *The Holy Qur'an—The All Giving Koraan* (koraan.info, as of October 9, 2016) (Q 1, 71–114, but only 1, 100–114 accessible online).

3. Ayoub, Mahmoud M., *The Awesome News, Interpretation of Juz' Amma—The Last Part of the Qur'an* (1997).

4. Cleary, Thomas, *The Essential Koran* (1993).

5. Haeri, Fadhlalla, *Beams of Illumination from the Divine Revelation: A Commentary (with Translation) of Juz'*

Amma, the Last Section of the Qur'an (1985), oft reprinted, most recently in 2008.

6. Helminski, Camille Adams, *The Light of Dawn: A Daybook of Verses from the Holy Qur'an* (1998).

7. Sells, Michael A., *Approaching the Qur'an: The Early Revelations* (1999/2001) (1, 53:1–8, 81–114).

8. Siddiqui, Abdul Hameed, *The Holy Qur'an: English Translation and Explanatory Notes* (1974). Only eight of thirty parts were produced prior to Siddiqui's death in 1974.

TWENTY-FIRST CENTURY (2000–2015)

1. Abdel Haleem, M.A.S., *The Qur'an: A New Translation* (2004). The best-selling recent translation of the Qur'an into English.

2. Ahamed, Syed Vickar, *The Glorious Qur'an: English Translation of the Meaning of the Message of the Quran* (1999 through 2013). Mostly derived, without acknowledgment, from Yusuf Ali (1937).

3. Ahmed, Nazeer, *The Qur'an* (2011), translated into American English.

4. Ahmed, Shabbir, *The Qur'an as It Explains Itself* (5th ed., 2012). An attempt to explain Qur'anic verses by cross-references within the Qur'an.

5. Ansari, Zafar Ishaq, *Towards Understanding the Qur'an* (2006), a later English translation of Maududi's *tafsir*.

6. Aziz, Hamid S., *The Meaning of the Holy Qur'an, with Explanatory Notes* (2000). Available online at www .islamawakened.com. It is said to be "not an original direct translation from the Arabic but the result of comparing several other English translations."

7. Bakhtiar, Laleh, *The Sublime Qur'an* (2007).

8. Birk, Sandow, *American Qur'an* (2015).

9. Busool, Assad Nimer, *The Wise Qur'an: A Modern English Translation* (2012).

10. Cleary, Thomas, *The Qur'an: A New Translation* (2004).

11. Dakok, Usama, *The Generous Qur'an* (2009).

12. Droge, A. J. *The Qur'an: A New Annotated Translation* (2013).

13. Eisabhai, Adam, *The Spirit of the Qur'an* (2006/2013), similar to a hardback Indian edition of Muhammad Asad.

14. Eisabhai, Adam, *The Message of the Qur'an* (2010, a paperback Indian edition of Muhammad Asad).

15. Elias, Afzal Hoosen, *Qur'an Made Easy* (2007).

16. Emerick, Yahya, *The Holy Qur'an: Guidance for Life* (2010).

17. Gohari, Mohammad Javad, *The Qur'an* (2002).

18. Hammad, Ahmed Zaki, *The Gracious Qur'an: A Modern Phrased Interpretation in English* (2007), with skillful use of half-bracket notations (more than 17,000) to make the text more accessible to non-Muslim, non-Arabic speakers/readers.

19. Hoque, Zohurul, *Translation and Commentary on the Holy Qur'an* (2000).

20. Islahi, Sayyid Hamed Abdul Rahman Alkaff, *The Simplified Qur'an (Simple Translation and Tafseer of the Glorious Qur'an)* (2013).

21. Itani, Talal, *Qur'an in English: Clear and Easy to Read* (2012).

22. Jones, Alan, *The Qur'an, Translated into English* (2007).

23. Kahveci, Niyazi, *English Translation of al-Qur'an al-Karim in Chronological Order* (2012).

24. Kaskas, Safi, *The Last Testament: A Translation of the Qur'an with References to the New and the Old*

Testaments a.k.a. *The Qur'an: A Contemporary Under-standing* (2015).

25. Khalidi, Tarif, *The Qur'an: A New Translation* (2008).

26. Khan, Wahiduddin, *The Qur'an: Translation and Commentary with Parallel Arabic Text* (2009). Published in India, but also widely disseminated without the Arabic text (also Goodword [2009]).

27. Khattab, Mustafa, *The Clear Qur'an: A Thematic English Translation* (2015) (the first Canadian translation of the Qur'an).

28. Kidwai, Abdur Raheem, *What Is in the Quran? Message of the Quran in Simple English* (2013).

29. McAuliffe, Jane, *The Qur'an* (Norton Critical Editions) (2017).

30. Moeinian, Bijan, *An Easy to Understand Translation of the Qur'an* (2005).

31. Nasr, Seyyed Hossein, *The Study Qur'an*, with Caner K. Dagli, Maria Massi Dakake, Joseph E. Lumbard, and Mohammed Rustom (2015).

32. Nooruddin Allamah, *The Holy Qur'an* (2005), an English rendition of Allamah's Urdu translation by Amatul Rahman Omar and Abdul Mannan.

33. Omar, Amatul Rahman, and Abdul Mannan Omar, *The Holy Qur'an: Arabic Text and English Translation* (2005).

34. Öztürk, A. Serdar, *Translation of the Qur'an* (2008).

35. Peachy, William Davut, and Manneh al-Johani, *The Qur'an: The Final Book of God—A Clear English Translation of the Glorious Qur'an* (2012/2014).

36. Qara'i, 'Ali Quli, *The Qur'an with a Phrase-by-Phrase English Translation* (2006).

37. Qaribullah, Hassan, and Ahmed Darwish, *The Meaning of the Glorious Qur'an* (2001), also available on tanzil.net.

38. Rahman, Muhammad Mustafizur, *The Holy Qur'an with English and Bengali Translation* (2014). Rendition into English of an earlier Bengali translation (1997).

39. Saffarzadeh, Tahere, *The Holy Qur'an—Persian and English Translation with Commentary* (bilingual edition, 2006/2011).

40. Shaikh, Shehnaz, and Kausar Khatri, *The Glorious Qur'an: Word-for-Word Translation to Facilitate Learning of Qur'anic Arabic* (2015).

41. Tahir ul-Qadri, Muhammad, *The Glorious Qur'an* (2011). Available in Arabic and English at http://www.irfan-ul -quran.com/quran/english (accessed on October 9, 2016).

42. Translation Committee, *The Majestic Qur'an*, translated by a committee that included Cambridge professor Timothy Winter, the American Muslim writer Uthman Hutchinson, and Mostafa al-Badawi (2000).

43. Unal, Ali, *The Qur'an with Annotated Interpretation in Modern English* (2008).

44. Usmani, Muhammad Taqi, *The Meaning of the Noble Qur'an (with Explanatory Notes in Two Volumes)* (2007).

45. Yuksel, Edip, with Layth Saleh al-Shaiban and Martha Schulte-Nafeh, *The Qur'an: A Monotheist Translation* (2012), a.k.a. *The Qur'an—A Pure and Literal Translation* (n.d., but likely 2008). See www.free-minds.org for a kindle edition preview of passages from the 2012 edition.

NOTABLE BUT PARTIAL TRANSLATIONS (SINCE 2000)

1. Ali, Muhammad Mohar, *A Word for Word Meaning of the Qur'an* (1998 to 2001; partial translation by Jamiyat Ihyaa Minhaaj Al Sunnah).

2. Khan, Irfan Ahmad, *Understanding the Qur'an: An Outline Study (with Translation) of the Last Thirty Divine Discourses* (2013).

3. Lings, Martin, *The Holy Qur'ān: Translations of Selected Verses* (2007).

4. Mir, Mustansir, *Understanding the Islamic Scripture: Selected Passages from the Qur'an, Translated and with Commentary* (2007).

5. Toorawa, Shawkat M., "'The Inimitable Rose,' Being Qur'anic *saj'* from *Sūrat al-Duhā* to *Sūrat al-Nās* (Q. 93–114) in English Rhyming Prose," *Journal of Qur'anic Studies* 8, no. 2 (2006): 143–56. "Referencing the Qur'an: A Proposal, with Illustrating Translations and Discussion (including translations of Ya Sin (Q. 36) and Fatiha (Q.1)," *Journal of Qur'anic Studies* 9, no. 1 (2007): 134–48. "*Surat Maryam* (Q. 19): Lexicon, Lexical Echoes, English Translation," *Journal of Qur'anic Studies* 13, no. 1 (2011): 25–78. "*Surat al-Raḥmān* (Q. 55), *Sūrat al-Aʿlā* (Q. 87), and *Sūrat al-Balad* (Q. 90), Translated into Cadenced, Rhyming English Prose," *Journal of Qur'anic Studies* 13, no. 2 (2011): 149–54.

NUMEROUS ONLINE RESOURCES FOR STUDYING THE QUR'AN

See chapter four, "The Virtual *Koran* and Beyond," for analysis of several sites, including tanzil.net, altafsir.org, alim.org, al-quran.info (accessed on October 9, 2016), and islamawakened.com. There is also a Qur'an database at http://www.qurandownload.com/ (accessed on October 9, 2016) and an independent website, http://www.englishtranslationsofthequran.com/translations.htm

(last updated June 2015 and accessed on October 9, 2016). It lists seventy-one *Koran* translations into English.

While al-quran.info (accessed on October 9, 2016) facilitates search of any verse among the 6,236 verses of the Qur'an in forty-one translations, one can only access five at a time. By contrast, islamawakened.com, with fifty-four translations, allows one to compare on a single page all fifty-four renditions of each *Koran*ic verse.

For serious sleuths of comparative translation efforts, there is no better online resource in 2017 than islamawakened.com.

PREFACE

1. For ease of reference, "the *Koran*" will often be used as shorthand for "the *Koran* in English" throughout the analysis that follows. It was due to the impact of George Sale's epochal work in the eighteenth century that "the *Koran*" became, and remains, the major name for English translations of al-Qur'an. For the extensive history of the transition—from Latin *Alchoran* to French *Alcoran* to English *The Koran*—see chapter 2, "The Orientalist *Koran*," and for its continuation in the twenty-first century, see chapter 7, "The Graphic *Koran*," for artist Sandow Birk's repeated use of *Koran* despite the title of his masterpiece: *American Qur'an* (New York: Liveright, 2015).

2. The translation here is taken from A. J. Arberry, *The Koran Interpreted* (New York: Macmillan, 1955).

   Arberry will be discussed at length in chapter 4 herein; he consistently renders "Qur'an" or "Arabic Qur'an" as "*Koran*" and "Arabic *Koran*" respectively. Except when quoting him or another translator directly, I will refer to Arabic *Qur'an* or Arabic al-Qur'an in my own analysis, in order to avoid confusing the reader, since the qualifier "Arabic" implies the original name "Qur'an" not the adopted English equivalent "*Koran*."

3. This rendition of Q 36, also provided on the cover, comes from the composite transcription of the American artist, Sandow Birk, treated at length in chapter 7. Birk self-consciously refers to *American Qur'an* in the title but then shifts to *Koran* or Arabic *Koran* in most of the text that follows; see especially Q 36 discussed in chapter 7. There is one exception: he does refer to Arabic Qur'an in Q 42:7a: "We have revealed to you an Arabic Qur'an." The choice here may be due to Birk's sensitivity that Q 42 "Council" refers to engagement with others, specifically Muslim others during the Iraq war (panel two).

4. The most astute, detailed argument against the orthodox view of the untranslatability of the Qur'an comes from Travis Zadeh, *The Vernacular Qur'an: Translation and the Rise of Persian Exegesis* (Oxford: Oxford University Press, 2012). The author skillfully shows how substitution and supplementation of the Arabic text were a frequent practice among Persian-speaking Muslims. He documents how interlinear translations were "entirely in keeping with how Muslims came to consider the Qur'an translatable," even though the interlinear version of scripture "does not serve as the ideal for all translation" (6). While recognizing the importance of vernacular culture that led to interlinear renditions of the Qur'an, it is only with free-standing translations, whether next to or apart from the Arabic text, that I am concerned for my analysis of the *Koran* in English.

5. This translation, like many to follow, comes from Thomas Cleary, *The Qur'an: A New Translation* (Chicago: Starlatch Press, 2004). Although my disagreements with Cleary are detailed in chapter 5,

"The *Koran* Up Close," the elegant simplicity of his rendition is commendable.

6. George Steiner, *After Babel: Aspects of Language and Translation* (New York: Oxford University Press, 1975), 310.

7. This insight was explored at length by a Duke University graduate student whom I had the privilege of teaching over twenty years ago. See F. V. Greifenhagen, "*Traduttore traditore*: An Analysis of the History of English Translations of the Qur'an," *Islam and Christian-Muslim Relations* 3, no. 2 (1992): 274–91.

8. I explored this issue—the Qur'an as verse yet not poetry—in an earlier essay, "Approximating *saj'* in English Renditions of the Qur'an: A Close Reading of Sura 93 (*al-Duha*) and the *basmala*," *Journal of Qur'anic Studies* 7, no. 1 (2005): 64–80.

9. Stefan Wild, "The Qur'an Today: Why Translate the Untranslatable?" Lecture delivered at Harvard University, October 28, 2010, and transcribed on http://www.bible-Qur'an.com/stefan-wild-why-translate-the-untranslatable/ (accessed on December 2, 2014).

10. Murad W. Hofmann, *Qur'an* (Istanbul: Çağrı Yayınları [Proselytizing Publishers], 2005), 59–60. The first three of these translators will be reviewed at length below; the full reference for them, as also for the fourth, can be found in the appendix: "The *Koran* in English by Author and Date." There are several other authors and analysts of Qur'an translation who echo Hofmann's defense of the untranslatability of the Qur'an. Among them is Hussein Abdul-Raof, *Qur'an Translation: Discourse, Texture, and Exegesis* (New York: Routledge, 2001), throughout but especially

p. 111, quoting several sources. Similar claims dot the Internet, e.g., this one at http://www.message4muslims .org.uk/the-Qur'an/english-translations.

The counterthesis, on the need to translate the Qur'an but with care, is offered in Ziad Almarsafy, *The Enlightenment Qur'an: The Politics of Translation and the Construction of Islam* (Oxford: Oneworld, 2009), especially with reference to English translations in the afterword, 185–93.

11. Adam F. Francisco, *Martin Luther and Islam: A Study in Sixteenth-Century Polemics and Apologetics* (Leiden: E. J. Brill, 2007), 103, 107, 237. Francisco's is a thorough, engaging study on Luther's attitude toward Islam, tracing both the sources and the contradictions implicit in the Protestant reformer's engagement with the Qur'an in Latin.

12. There was a single translation, by Ross, in the seventeenth century, but it was from French into English. Sale in many ways counts as the pioneer translator of the Qur'an from Arabic into English. See chapter 2 herein, and also Zadeh, *Vernacular Qur'an*, 7: "the first English translation based on the original Arabic was produced in 1734 by George Sale."

13. Indeed, it was not until the twenty-first century that we find the first Arabic-speaking scholars, Muslim and non-Muslim, making commercially promoted, freestanding translations of the *Koran* into English. In the appendix, note, e.g., N. J. Dawood (1956), an Iraqi Jewish scholar, and much later, Tariq Khalidi (2008), a Lebanese Muslim scholar.

14. Jalaluddin Rumi, *Signs of the Unseen: The Discourses of Jalaluddin Rumi*, trans. W. M. Thackston Jr. (Putney,

VT: Threshold Books, 1994), 85–86. I am indebted to Professor Omid Safi for calling my attention to this reference.

15. Cleary, *The Qur'an: A New Translation*, but with modifications to eliminate Cleary's use of "God" in every instance where the Arabic pronoun "*hu*/He" appears. See the pervasive reference to Cleary in the newest version of the *Koran* in English: Sandow Birk, *American Qur'an* (2015), analyzed in chapter 7 herein, "The Graphic *Koran*."

16. Ibn Khaldun, *The Muqaddimah*, trans. Franz Rosenthal (1967, 2005; Princeton, NJ: Princeton University Press, 2015), 47–48. Two recent works in the domain of world history and philosophy of religion confirm the enduring importance of polytheism. Yuval Noah Harari, in *Sapiens: A Brief History of Humankind* (London: Harvill Secker, 2014) underscores polytheism as the foundational religion of humankind (chapter 12), while Robert Wright, in *The Evolution of God* (New York: Little, Brown, 2009), argues that the *Koran*ic accent on the Divine Other was premised on the challenge of polytheistic resistance to a unitary supreme power. Moreover, it was the struggle between polytheistic views and monotheistic counterclaims that fueled the moral imagination of the early Muslim movement, allying it with Christian and Jewish neighbors at the same time as their leaders forged a distinctive polity within and beyond Arabia. The *Koran* provided, in Wright's words, "God's phonetic footprints" for the adherents of a new and rigorous monotheism (341–43), so much so that in ensuing struggles with polytheists the *Koran* expanded the

arc of salvation, making it "unrivaled as a revelation attesting to the correlation between circumstance and moral consciousness" (405).

17. I am deliberately spelling muslims with a small "m," to indicate those who accept and acknowledge prophetic revelation, whether they be Muslims (belonging to Islam) or muslims (having some other scripture, whether Hindus, Buddhists, Sikhs, Christians, or Jews, that defines their law and revealed way). On the large-scale effort to convert all "barbarians" to Christianity or Islam, see the Pew Research Poll of 2010: http://www.pewforum.org/2010/04/15/executive-summary-islam-and-christianity-in-sub-saharan-africa/, and anecdotally, Eliza Griswold, *The Tenth Parallel: Dispatches on the Fault Line between Christianity and Islam* (New York: Farrar, Straus and Giroux, 2010).

18. Muhammad Abdel Haleem, *The Qur'an* (2004), slightly expanded to emphasize that "the people" are those who accept prophecy, and divided into two lines to indicate stress.

19. The appendix herein provides an extensive, but not exhaustive, listing of *Koran* translations. I am just counting full translations into English that I have been able to track down during the past five years. There are others that I have not found, and there are also partial translations that are deemed worthy of attention. In assessing some works as plagiarism, I have often made my judgment based on a side-by-side comparison of texts, but I have also benefited from the careful work of Abdur Raheem Kidwai, *Translating the Untranslatable—A Critical Guide to 60 English Translations of the Quran* (2011). Formerly available free

online, it can now be purchased through eswar.com, India's biggest e-book shop, at http://www.eswar.com/book.htm?bookcode=0080145.

20. See chapter 3, "The South Asian *Koran*," for a detailed account of Yusuf Ali, his life and his work.

21. It is ironic that Yusuf Ali's own translation and commentary are later altered to conform to "orthodox" standards imposed by monitors in Saudi Arabia. See chapter 5, "The Politics of *Koran* Translation."

22. G. Willow Wilson, an American Muslim, provides an in-depth review in the *Washington Post* on January 21, 2016. "'*American Qur'an*' Is an Old/New Masterpiece," she notes; "its flaws only serve its virtuosity." See https://www.washingtonpost.com/entertainment/books/american-quran-is-an-oldnew-masterpiece/2016/01/21/c067c350-becd-11e5-9443-7074c3645405_story.html. For a more critical review, see Holland Cotter, "Sandow Birk: 'American Qur'an,'" *New York Times*, September 17, 2010, at http://www.nytimes.com/2010/09/17/arts/design/17galleries-002-001.html?_r=0. Cotter's was a mid-work review; there has not yet (as of June 2016) been a review of the final work from the *New York Times*. The cautionary tone of Cotter's piece seems to stem from some warnings that appeared in an earlier, decidedly more upbeat review of Birk's work by another *New York Times* critic, Jori Finkel. See "'Personal Meditations' on the *Koran*," *New York Times*, August 28, 2009. Neither essay explores the balance of visual versus literary translation that is at the heart of Birk's endeavor, a balance that is both detected and demonstrated in Wilson's review.

CHAPTER 1   Muhammad and Revelation

1. The biography that follows is adapted from my earlier book, *The Qur'an: A Biography* (New York: Atlantic, 2006), 21–49. I am well aware of other, more experimental approaches to the life of Muhammad. They have been brilliantly outlined in Kecia Ali, *The Lives of Muhammad* (Cambridge, MA: Harvard University Press, 2014). The South Asian impress is as evident there as in the translation activity of the twentieth, and now twenty-first century. Some of them involve the same players, that is, the *Koran* translators were also Prophet biographers. Since the scope of my inquiry would be vastly expanded if I were to account for all these developments, I have limited myself to the traditional profile, the one familiar to most *Koran* translators and commentators. I have also refrained from depicting the Prophet Muhammad either as a skilled team manager or a model CEO, though both perspectives are noted in my review of Ali's book, "A Muhammad for Every Age," *Chronicle Review*, October 10, 2014, B13.

2. For more than a decade, there has been a lively debate about the critical text of the Qur'an. It revolves around the Uthmanic codex of 634, but also the Al-Azhar approved standard edition of the Arabic Qur'an in 1924. This debate has led at least one thoughtful observer to conclude: "The formation of a standard, single text of the *Qur'ān* seems to be much more complicated than the traditional Muslim account which maintains that the text was fixed during the Caliphate of 'Uthmān" (Timothy Conway at http://www

.enlightened-spirituality.org/Qur'an_quotes.html, accessed on December 7, 2014). This polite skepticism is also confirmed in the recent full-length study by the leading European authority on Qur'an texts: Francois Deroche, *Qur'ans of the Umayyads: A First Overview* (Leiden: E. J. Brill, 2013). Since all the translations under review accept the standard Al-Azhar approved text, I will not engage this issue in what follows.

3. Each passage entails reflection and choice on which translation to follow. In order to unclutter the narrative, I have detailed my preference for the translations I selected in endnotes; my special preference is for the alliterative patterns of Shawkat Toorawa in those passages that he has rendered into English.

4. This translation illustrates the ongoing difficulty of relying on any extant translation of the *Koran* into English for capturing the sense of the Arabic Qur'an. It begins with Cleary, *The Qur'an: A New Translation*, slightly modified, but then instead of his rendering for the second part, I have preferred the twist of Yusuf Ali, *The Holy Qur'an: Text, Translation and Commentary*, with a slight variation on the first verb "incline to them" instead of "love to them."

5. Here my preferred source for the *Koran* in English is Jones, *The Qur'an, Translated into English*, though he adds a copulative in the final line, which I have removed.

6. This exchange is adopted from Ibn Ishaq, *The Life of Muhammad*, trans. A. Guillaume (1955; Karachi: Oxford University Press 1970), 105–7. It is repeated in almost every commentary on Q 96:1–5, with particular stress on Khadija's role in convincing Muhammad

(a) he was not, as he at first thought, mad, and also (b) that he should accept the divine commission/ challenge issued by the Angel Gabriel. I've modified Guillaume's rendition, replacing "read" with "recite," to reflect the oral nature of revelation in the Qur'an. I've also added the comparison to Jeremiah. The actual Koran translation here is the first of many from Shawkat Toorawa, to whom I am indebted on many counts as friend, advisor, and colleague. Most of the Koran citations that follow also come from Shawkat M. Toorawa, "'The Inimitable Rose,' Being Qur'anic *saj'* from *Sūrat al-Duhā* to *Sūrat al-Nās* (Q. 93–114) in English Rhyming Prose," *Journal of Qur'anic Studies* 8, no. 2 (2006): 143–56.

7. An anonymous poet cited in Shaykh Nizam Ad-Din Awliya, *Morals for the Heart* (Conversations of Shaykh Nizam ad-din Awliya recorded by Amir Hasan Sijzi), trans. Bruce B. Lawrence (Mahwah, NJ: Paulist Press, 1992), 314.

8. See Muhammad Asad, *The Message of the Qur'an* (London: Book Foundation, 2009), appendix 4, for a review of conflicting interpretations, all of which, however, agree that the event depicted occupies a crucial place in the emergence, and persistence, of Muhammad as God's final prophet.

9. Toorawa, "The Inimitable Rose."

10. Ibid.

11. Ibid.

12. Ibid.

13. Cleary, *The Qur'an: A New Translation*, with some modifications: "Book," instead of "scripture," "all creation" instead of "all worlds," and not using "God" but

instead retaining the pronoun "He" from the Arabic Qur'an.

14. This is undoubtedly the most crucial and contested of all passages from the *Koran* in English. In the Arabic Qur'an, *al-Fatiha* or the Opening is the sole passage that is required in daily prayer, and so it is fair to say, as does Mustansir Mir among others, that it bears comparison with the Lord's Prayer. Especially if one omits the last part of the Lord's Prayer, "For thine is the Kingdom, the Power, and the Glory forever and ever," as does Luke, then each is framed by invocation of the Highest Name, followed by sparse but critical petitions from the humble servant, the "ordinary" believer. Mustansir Mir, *Understanding the Islamic Scripture* (New York: Longman, 2008), 18–19. Again, this rhymed version is provided by Shawkat Toorawa, and bears comparison with several other versions reviewed in chapter 5, "The *Koran* Up Close" and chapter 7, "The Graphic *Koran*."

15. Shawkat M. Toorawa, "Referencing the Qur'an: A Proposal, with Illustrative Translations and Discussion (including translations of Ya Sin [Q.36] and Fatiha [Q.1])," *Journal of Qur'anic Studies* 9, no. 1 (2007): 134–48.

16. Here I have preferred the rendition of Pickthall, though with Allah translated as God and archaic prepositions or adverbs eliminated, then replaced by their contemporary equivalents.

17. Even though Ahmed Ali (1988) is seldom listed among the foremost *Koran* translators, he has captured the nuance of this critical verse (Q 2:217) better than others, at least in my view. To compare his rendition with fifty other choices, please consult

the most comprehensive verse-by-verse, chapter-by-chapter online Qur'an/*Koran* website, http://www.islamawakened.com/quran/2/217/default.htm, accessed on August 19, 2016, and discussed in chapter 4, "The Virtual *Koran*."

18. In this instance I have provided my own translation, culling together phrases from several renditions of Q 3:123–26.

19. Paraphrased from Ibn Ishaq, *Life of Muhammad*, 386.

20. See http://www.islamawakened.com/Qur'an/29/57/default.htm (accessed on October 9, 2016), where the translation most closely approximates that from *Tafhim al-Qur'an* by Abul A'la Maududi, rendered from Urdu into English by Zafar Ishaq Ansari.

CHAPTER 2 The Orientalist *Koran*

1. Steiner, *After Babel*, 266. Also cited in Greifenhagen, "*Traduttore traditore*," 274–91. As mentioned in the preface, Greigenhagen's essay provides multiple insights into the trajectory and the perplexity of numerous efforts to translate the Arabic Qur'an into the English *Koran*.

2. Since 1978, almost all academic discussion of Orientalism has focused on the subject of cultural imperialism, as distinct from exploratory scholarship, regarding the Muslim world generally but especially the Middle East. A temporal divide occurred in 1978 because of Edward Said's landmark work *Orientalism* (New York: Pantheon Books, 1978). Said himself stressed that "Islam became an image . . . whose function was not so much to represent Islam in itself as to represent it for the medieval Christian" (60). But some Orientalists

were able to be both devout Christians and open-minded scholars. That perspective pervades most of the *Koran* translators here discussed and described as Orientalist. It is crucial to note that despite their Christian allegiances, they do not disregard what Muslims themselves thought of the Qur'an, even when they project what Hamid Algar has decried as "Judeo-Christian theological animus toward Islam." Hamid Algar, "The Study of Islam: The Work of Henry Corbin," *Religious Studies Review* 6, no. 2 (1980): 85.

3. *Lex Mahumet pseudorprophete que arabice Alchoran—The Religion of Muhammad the Pseudo-Prophet and the Arabic Koran.* The title shift seems to have been seamless: Qaf (*q*) in Arabic is at first replaced with *ch*, then *c*, and eventually *k*, while *u* becomes *o*. Mark of Toledo, *Liber Alchorani* (1211), imitates Robert, while three centuries later, Iohannes Gabriel Terrolensis gives his (unpublished) translation the title *Alcoranus* (1511), and Theodore Bibliander's mid-sixteenth-century printed editions of Robert (1543/1550) give the shorter name *Alcoran*, and L. Marracci in the seventeenth century follows suit titling his diligent work *Alcorani textus universus*. Both French and Italian later translations retain Alcoran, while German and English translators prefer Der *Koran* or the *Koran*, respectively. Sale, as we will see below, sets the standard for all who follows when he titles his 1734 work *The Koran, Commonly Called The Alcoran of Mohammed.*

4. James Kritzeck, *Peter the Venerable and Islam* (Princeton, NJ: Princeton University Press, 1964), 161. The reference to Kritzeck, and several other features of this chapter, draw on my earlier work, *The Qur'an: A*

Biography (New York: Atlantic Books, 2006), chapter 7. I am indebted to Kritzeck for having introduced me to the study of Islamic philosophy and *Koran*ic translation in the late 1950s; it is to him that I dedicate this book.

5. Thomas E. Burman, *Reading the Qur'an in Latin Christendom, 1140–1560* (Philadelphia: University of Pennsylvania Press, 2007), 15. In full praise of Ketton's translation, Burman notes: "Ketton's translation would go on to become the most widely read Latin version of Islam's holy book. It survives in some twenty-five medieval and early modern manuscripts and would be printed in editions of 1543 and 1550. When European Christians read the Qur'an any time between the mid-twelfth and late seventeenth century, they usually read Robert's version." Also relevant and of value for understanding Robert's impact is Thomas E. Burman, "Tafsir and Translation: Traditional Qur'an Exegesis and the Latin Qur'ans of Robert of Ketton and Mark of Toledo," *Speculum* 73 (1998): 703–22. The further impact of Robert's translation after its publication in print has been charted by Hartmut Bobzin, "'A Treasuring of Heresies': Christian Polemics against the *Koran*," in *The Qur'an as Text*, ed. Stefan Wild (Leiden: E. J. Brill, 1996), 156–75.

6. Adam F. Francisco, *Martin Luther and Islam: A Study in Sixteenth-Century Polemics and Apologetics* (Leiden: E. J. Brill, 2007), 103. Francisco's is a thorough, engaging study on Luther's attitude toward Islam. On the one hand, Luther was firmly opposed to the "demonic and apocalyptic" ideology of the Turks, considering Turks to be "completely repugnant servants of the

Devil" (236), yet he also argued that one must know the Qur'an in Latin since "it is of value for the learned to read the writings of the enemy" (107).

7. Burman, *Reading the Qur'an*, 35.

8. Ibid.

9. Jefferson's fascination with Islam, as well as his use of the Sale translation, is analyzed in Denise Spellberg, *Thomas Jefferson's Qur'an: Islam and the Founders* (New York: Vintage. 2014).

10. Zaid Elmarasafy, *The Enlightenment Qur'an: The Politics of Translation and the Construction of Islam* (Oxford: Oneworld, 2009), 23. Elmarsafy's detailed exploration of Sale's relationship to Marracci is invaluable for understanding the intra-Christian rivalry between Protestants (that is, Anglicans) and Catholics, in relating to the Arabic Qur'an and its message, whether in Latin (Marracci) or English (Sale).

11. E. Denison Ross, introduction to G. Sale, *The Koran—Translated into English from the Original Arabic* (London: Frederick Warne, 1927), viii.

12. For more on the literary qualities of Sale's translation, especially in comparison and contrast with Marracci, see Elmarsafy, *Enlightenment Qur'an*, passim but especially 47–63.

13. Ibid., 71–72.

14. See Alexander Bevilacqua, "The Qur'an Translations of Marracci and Sale," *Journal of the Warburg and Courtauld Institutes* 76 (2013): 119.

15. Ibid., 129–30 (emphasis added). I am indebted to Bevilacqua for his generous discussion of this project during e-mail exchanges in early 2015.

16. Rodwell, *The Koran*, vii.

17. Ibid., 13.

18. For a major example of Rodwell's enduring appeal, see my analysis of *American Qur'an* in chapter 7, "The Graphic *Koran*."

19. Muhammad Baqir Behbudi and Colin Turner, trans., *The Qur'an: A New Interpretation* (London: Curzon Press, 1997), x.

CHAPTER 3   The South Asian *Koran*

1. Art critic Gregory Sholette spoke about marginalized artists as crucial to mainstream artists. Alluding to dark matter in the universe, well known to astrophysicists, Sholette observed in 2011 that "Marginalised artists provide the 'dark matter' of the art world. They are essential to the survival of the mainstream, and it is due to their unacknowledged labor that imagination and creativity in the art world originate and thrive in the non-commercial sector shut off from prestigious galleries." Gregory Sholette, *Dark Matter: Art and Politics in the Age of Enterprise Culture* (London: Pluto Press, 2011), 1. Less cutthroat than art dealers, but no less commercially minded, major twentieth-century publishers have supported certain *Koran* translations, creating a hierarchy of value that pervades reader expectations about the English *Koran*. More importantly, most readers of the *Koran* in English are simply unaware of the extent to which the few heralded translations mask the effort, and often the creativity, of the many other dedicated scholars, both Muslim and non-Muslim, who have produced partial or complete *Koran* translations. See the appendix for a full listing of these oft-forgotten or marginally cited names.

2. Bibliographic descriptions of each are provided in the appendix.

3. Abdur Raheem Kidwai, *From Darkness into Light: Life and Works of Maulana Abdul Majid Daryabadi* (Springs, South Africa: Ahsan Publications, 2013), 51.

4. Ibid., 54.

5. Ibid., 106, and then later, without further comment, Kidwai also notes that Daryabadi "did not endorse the consensus view that Qadiyanis stand outside the fold of Islam. He believed that the tendency of declaring anyone a non-Muslim should be discouraged" (269). The filter of orthodoxy was clearly less strong for Daryabadi than the anvil of history.

6. The Ahmadi movement became internally divided after Ghulam Ahmad Qadiani's death in 1908. There emerged two main factions of Ahmadis: one, from Qadian, claiming that he was not only a messiah but also a prophet, the other, from Lahore, making the more modest claim that he was merely a *mujaddid* or renewer. For insight into the debate and the internal schism it produced, see Yohanan Friedmann, *Prophecy Continuous: Aspects of Ahmadi Religious Thought and Its Medieval Background* (Berkeley: University of California Press, 1989), 147–51. While it is clear that Muhammad Ali initially did attribute some form of prophetic office to Ghulam Ahmad Qadiani, it is equally clear that by the late 1930s he had renounced any such association of prophecy with Ghulam Ahmad, separating himself fully and unqualifiedly from the Qadian branch of the Ahmadiyya. Muhammad Ali's critics do not acknowledge the significance of this split, preferring to deride all Ahmadis as equally heretical.

7. Hafiz Ghulam Sarwar, *Translation of the Holy Qur'an: From the Original Arabic Text with Critical Essays, Life of Muhammad, Complete Summary of Contents*, 2nd ed. (Karachi: National Book Foundation, 1973), xxxvii.

8. Ibid., xlii. Many readers with knowledge of the Arabic Qur'an will be surprised at this translation of Q 12:76. It comes at the juncture in Sura Yusuf where Joseph is about to foil his brothers' attempt to hide their role in having sold him to the Egyptians. Muhammad Ali translates this verse: "And above everyone possessed of knowledge is the All-Knowing One (i.e., God)." But Ghulam Sarwar treats the final participle as self-referential (ibid., 138). In this choice he is following his Orientalist precursors—Sale, Rodwell, and Palmer—but not Muhammad Ali or the majority of subsequent Muslim translators.

9. For this depiction, as also for several elements in the pen portraits I provide of Muhammad Ali, Marmaduke Pickthall and Yusuf Ali, I have benefited from the collegial friendship of Brett Wilson. Brett began as my graduate student over a decade ago, and has since blossomed into a first-rate scholar of early Republican Turkey, with special focus on Turkish translations of the Qur'an. From his monograph, *Translating the Qur'an in an Age of Nationalism: Print Culture and Modern Islam in Turkey* (London: Oxford University Press, 2015), I have drawn both lucid insights and biographical descriptions provided in his chapter 6, "Caliph and Qur'an: English Translations, Egypt and the Search for a Centre." My own stress is on the South Asian theater rather than the Anatolian peninsula,

but *Koran* translations connect both to the global movement depicted in this chapter. For an extended depiction of Muhammad Ali, see Wilson, *Translating the Qur'an*, 190–96.

10. Wilson, *Translating the Qur'an*, 195.

11. Rim Hassen, "English Translations of the Qur'an by Women: Different or Derived?" (Department of English and Comparative Literature, University of Warwick, 2012), 123, is the source for this reference, and also the insight it conveys.

12. The number of editions, and the often perverse modifications of Yusuf Ali's original text, have been traced by M. A. Sherif, *Searching for Solace: A Biography of Abdullah Yusuf Ali, Interpreter of the Qur'an* (1994; Selang, Malaysia: Islamic Book Trust, 2004), 224–29. Critical assessments of Saudi officialdom and its role in the modified versions are provided in Bruce B. Lawrence, "Abdullah Yusuf Ali's Translation of the Qur'an: An 80-Year Retrospective with Special Attention to Surat ad-Duha (Q 93)," KA Nizami Centre for Qur'anic Studies, Aligarh Muslim University, Aligarh (2013).

13. Quoted from Yusuf Ali, *The Holy Qur'an*, ix, and cited in Wilson, *Translating the Qur'an*, 206.

14. Marmaduke Pickthall, "Mr. Yusuf Ali's Translation of the Qur'an," *Islamic Culture* 9 (1935): 519–21. Like the quotation above, and much commentary from this section, it is adroitly presented in Wilson, *Translating the Qur'an*, 207.

15. See below for an extended commentary on the misappropriation of Yusuf Ali by Saudi officialdom. I elaborate on this aberration in my earlier essay, Lawrence, "Abdullah Yusuf Ali's Translation of the Qur'an," 28–33.

16. Professor Omid Safi wrote me that "Umar Faruq Abd-Allah, who has been steadily rising to become one of the major *shuyukh* (leaders) of American Islam, respected both for his scholarly knowledge and by his followers for his *baraka*, has been leading tours to the grave site of both Yusuf Ali and Pickthall." E-mail received on May 24, 2016.

17. This quotation/translation of Q 102 "Greed for More and More" is clearly anachronistic. It is from Asad's own later translation, but I have never been able to trace which earlier English translation he read in 1926. The reference in Q 112:8 to "boon," rather than to "pleasures," "joys," "bliss," "bounties," "favors," or "blessings" found in several translations, suggests a link to Muhammad Ali. Of earlier translators, only Muhammad Ali renders *an-na'im* as "boons," and since there are other methodological parallels between Muhammad Ali and Muhammad Asad in their approach to *Koran* translation, and since we know that the Ahmadis by the 1920s had translated the *Koran* into German as well as English, Muhammad Ali is a likely source for Asad's early attraction to this chilling and compelling Qur'anic passage.

18. Muhammad Asad (Leopold Weiss), *The Road to Mecca* (New York: Simon and Schuster, 1954), 329–31.

19. *The Guardian*, 1980, a quotation that I have not been able to trace further.

20. Among the most notable who follow the English-only model are A. J. Arberry, T. J. Irving, N. J. Dawood, Alan Jones, Tarif Khalidi, Muhammad Abdel Haleem, and Thomas Cleary. All of their translations have been cited in the appendix.

21. Yet Hasan Gai Eaton, who wrote a prologue to the 2003 edition of *The Message of the Qur'an*, notes that both Muhammad Ali and Picthall [*sic*] are two preceding translators with whom to compare elements of Asad's translation (i).

22. Peter Clarke, *Marmaduke Pickthall: British Muslim* (London: Quartet, 1986), 67.

23. Mohammed Marmaduke Pickthall, *The Meaning of the Glorious Koran: An Explanatory Translation* (London: Alfred A. Knopf, 1930), vii.

24. Abdullah Yusuf Ali. Cited from the first edition of *The Holy Qur'an* (Hertfordshire, UK: Wordsworth, 2000), xi.

25. Muhammad Asad, *The Message of the Qur'an*, viii–x.

CHAPTER 4   The Virtual *Koran* and Beyond

1. Gary Bunt, *iMuslims: Rewiring the House of Islam* (Chapel Hill: University of North Carolina Press, 2009), 83–84.

2. Dr. Abdul Hamid Othman quoted in *The New Strait Times*, July 13, 1996, 2.

3. See chapter 3, 65–80.

4. Numerous examples can be found at https://en .wikipedia.org/wiki/English_translations_of_the _Quran, accessed on October 24, 2015. *The Clarion Cry of the Eternal Qur-aan*, for instance, I could only find on the Wikipedia site, while the final item, traced to Thomas McElwain, is unavailable even on Amazon.com.

5. Anthony H. Johns and Suha Taji-Farouki, "Chapter 8—Appendix: The Qur'an in English, in *The Qur'an and Its Readers World-Wide: Contemporary*

Commentaries and Translations, ed. Suha Taji-Farouki
(Oxford: Oxford University Press, 2016). Cited from
a draft version, alas never published.

6. Excerpted from *Studies in Comparative Religion*,
   Arberry obituary, available at http://www.studiesin
   comparativereligion.com/public/authors/%20AJ
   _Arberry.aspx, last accessed on January 22, 2016.

7. Arberry, *The Koran Interpreted* (introduction), 25–26.

8. http://al-quran.info/pages/language/english. The
   efficiency of this website conceals its redundancy of
   information and judgmental incompetence. Although
   less sophisticated, altafsir.com and islamawakened
   .com, are far more reputable, and the last is a laudably
   inclusive site for making broad comparisons of both
   individual verses and translators' styles.

9. See https://www.facebook.com/iconverttoislam/posts
   /838691726179789:0, accessed on October 24, 2015.

10. See for instance the critique in Kidwai, *Translating the
    Untranslatable*, #56 (276–81).

11. Cited from a personal e-mail received in January 2014.

12. Michael Sells, *Approaching the Qur'an: The Early Rev-
    elations* (Ashland, OR: White Cloud Press, 1999), 215.
    Also see chapter 6, "The Politics of *Koran* Translation,"
    n. 11, for more on Sells and his pioneering work.

13. A colleague has reported: "The Umm Muhammed
    version is widely printed, with paperbacks being dis-
    tributed at many *da'wa* events, and given away in the
    streets: I got free copies in east London!" Gary Bunt,
    personal communication, November 11, 2015.

14. For an extensive analysis of Tahereh Saffarzadeh, as
    also Umm Muhammad and Laleh Bakhtiar, see the
    probing, insightful thesis of Rim Hassen, "English

Translations of the Qur'an by Women: Different or Derived?" (Department of English and Comparative Literature, University of Warwick, 2012). The other woman cited in her analysis is the Sufi author and translator Camille Helminski, whose partial translation, *The Light of Dawn*, appeared in 1999. Since the principal focus of my own analysis is full translations into English, I have explored neither Helminski nor the French translators Fatma Zaida and Denise Masson, also treated in Hassen's pioneering work, but a bibliographic citation for Helminski is given in the appendix.

15. As Bakhtiar explains in the preface, although her mother was American and her father Iranian, she was raised in the United States in a single parent household.

16. For numerous examples, see Kidwai, *Translating the Untranslatable* #31 (146–47).

17. First published in Malaysia as *Qur'an and Woman* in 1992, this classic work has since been renamed *Qur'an and Woman: Reading the Sacred Text from a Woman's Perspective* and reprinted by Oxford University Press in 1999. It remains for nearly all scholars the most incisive, feminist reading of the Qur'an.

18. See Andreas Christmann, "Reading the Qur'an in Germany: Contemporary Muslim German Interpretations of Qur'an 4: 34," in Taji-Farouki, *The Qur'an and Its Readers World-Wide: Contemporary Commentaries and Translation*. Christmann explores how the interpretive strategies of contemporary German translators attempt to limit its punitive aspects, producing choices (most paralleling Yusuf Ali's [*Holy*

Qur'an]) that project an authentic, pristine Islam free from the misogynist views of later translators and commentators.

19. Recently, one Muslim feminist scholar has raised the prospect that no reading of the Qur'an, and Q 4:34 in particular, can satisfy the demand for gender justice, but she encourages all Muslim women to pursue "uncertainty as a mercy in the face of the undaunting finality of certainty and the permanence of its limits." Aysha A. Hidayatullah, *Feminist Edges of the Qur'an* (New York: Oxford University Press, 2014). Yet that approach leaves open to challenge not just the certainty of Q 4:34 but of all juridically weighted passages from the Qur'an.

CHAPTER 5   The *Koran* Up Close

1. See koraan.info for Ibrahim Abu Nab's original, unprecedented rendition of the final forty-three chapters, Q 71–114, as well as Q 1, al-Fatiha, along with an introductory essay outlining his approach to the aural as well as the literary meaning of the Qur'an. I have benefited from his insight, his creativity, and, above all, his generosity in the brief period from our first meeting in 1986 till his untimely death in 1991.

2. I have modified the tense and syntax here to make the phrase fit the tone of this strong recommendation for all Qur'an/*Koran* translation.

3. Navid Kermani, *God Is Beautiful: The Aesthetic Experience of the Qur'an* (Cambridge: Polity Press, 2014), 193, 81. Kermani's entire book is teeming with insight into the deeply literary and lyrical quality of the Qur'an in its own terms, a revelation but one

linked to poetry since "poetry was the only medium besides revelation (and, later mysticism) with an acknowledged claim to association with a transcendental reality" (288). The age-old prejudice against poetry, and against any link of the Qur'an to poetry, continues in many translations, even by broad-gauged, well-intentioned scholars, e.g., Ahmad Zaki Hammad, *The Gracious Qur'an* (Lisle, IL: Lucent Interpretations, 2007), 1189: "To liken the Qur'an to poetry is not only fundamentally wrong, but demeaning of its Heavenly Revelation."

4. In addition to the vast commentary literature about the Fatiha, there is now also the discussion of this pivotal chapter in Angelika Neuwirth, *Scripture, Poetry, and the Making of a Community: Reading the Qur'an as a Literary Text* (Oxford: Oxford University Press, 2014), chapter 8, "Surat al-Fatiha (Q.1): Opening of the Textual Corpus of the Qur'an or Introit of the Prayer Service."

5. Kermani, *God Is Beautiful*, 222. Kermani explains how focus on individual verses does not invalidate the value of the Qur'an as a complete work. From an aesthetic perspective, however, "the structure of the work is not relevant: the quality of the Qur'an is judged from the findings on its individual verse." He quickly adds that some suras, or chapters, such as Q 12 Surah Yusuf and Q 55 Surat al-Rahman are of inimitable quality, due to their structure, but the judgment of musical, literary quality has to do with smaller units, individual verses. The molecular quality of the Qur'an has been recognized by some Muslim scholars but very few Western scholars, of whom Norman O. Brown ("The

Apocalypse of Islam," regarding Q 18) is the exception. See Brown, "The Apocalypse of Islam," *Social Text* 8 (Winter 1983–84): 155–71.

6. Note several references to Toorawa in the appendix, where three of his formative articles containing translations from the Qur'an in rhymed prose are cited. He is also noted with gratitute in my acknowledgments.

7. Following Muhammad Ali, Pickthall in the original 1930 edition does not number the *basmala*, though El-'Ashi, his recent editor, does so in keeping with Sunni Orthodox practice. See the edited update of Pickthall (*Meaning of the Glorious Koran: An Explanatory Translation*, 1996). John Bowen summarizes the dilemma deftly when he observes: "There are two well-known English versions of the Qur'an: Yusuf Ali's counts the *basmala* as a verse: Pickthall's does not (the two translators parse differently, and thus each depicts the chapter as having seven verses, a highly valued number)." John Richard Bowen, *Muslims through Discourse: Religion and Ritual in Gayo Society* (Princeton, NJ: Princeton University Press, 1993), 307. The issue continues to occupy commentators until today, but most side with Yusuf Ali and others in counting the *basmala* as a verse in the Opening sura but not elsewhere in the other 113 suras of the Noble Book. See also below, n. 11.

8. In a note, Toorawa explains that he reverses the two Divine names, Ar-Rahman and Ar-Rahim, in order to achieve rhyme in English. See Shawkat M. Toorawa, "Referencing the Qur'an: A Proposal, with Illustrating Translations and Discussion (Including Translations of Ya Sin (Q.36) and Fatiha (Q.1)," *Journal of Qur'anic Studies* 9, no. 1 (2007): 147.

9. All of these choices are an advance over Sale, for despite the good will that one can see in his commentary, as discussed at length by Elmarsafy, there is the issue of Marracci's actual translations. Al-Fatiha in its initial verses becomes:

> IN THE NAME OF THE MOST
> MERCIFUL GOD.
> PRAISE be to God, the Lord of all creatures; the most Merciful, the king of the day of judgment.

Here the two attributes—*rahman* and *rahim*—are collapsed into one, as if their complementarity amounted to redundancy, requiring only one translation for both. *'Alamain*, which can be worlds or universe, instead becomes "creatures," again with a reduction in scope of the intent of the Arabic text, and then the role of Allah/God at the end of time is reflected in no caps as "the king of the day of judgment." In short, Marracci's is at once an inept and demeaning rendition of the core Qur'anic text for ritual and belief.

10. This is to indicate the first *juz'* or section used for reciting in Arabic, in this case extending up to Q 2:141, not quite halfway through Surat al-Baqarah, the longest of the Qur'anic suras/chapters with 286 verses. Other than Irving, who was chided for doing so, no other major translator has deemed to make the *Koran* in English explicitly worthy of ritual observance, and Irving was, of course, criticized for this as also for his implication that an American version, like the KJV of the Bible, was authorizing its use independently of the source language, Arabic.

11. This alternate counting, of course, poses a major hurdle for online Qur'an search engines. They must have standardized entries for each verse, so none of them can, or does, indicate how early Pickthall, like M. Muhammad Ali, did not count the initial *basmala* of the Opening chapter, and so had to divide into two the final verse (*sirat* until the end), which in all other translations is rendered as a single unit.

12. In what follows all the frame elements are omitted, in order to highlight and compare the verbal choices for each translation.

13. Shawkat M. Toorawa, "'The Inimitable Rose,' Being Qur'anic *saj'* from *Sūrat al-Duhā* to *Sūrat al-Nās* (Q. 93–114) in English Rhyming Prose," *Journal of Qur'anic Studies* 8, no. 2 (2006): 143–56.

14. A. J. Arberry, *The Koran Interpreted* (New York: Macmillan, 1955), 25.

15. I hesitated to include my own collaborative effort in this chapter, or in the book as a whole, since it is still in the early phases. Both Professor Rafey Habib (Rutgers) and I are committed to producing a verse rendition of the entire Qur'an, but that remains a distant goal, not likely to be completed before 2019 since we, like our predecessors, have found the challenge of *Koran* translation at once alluring and daunting. When done, our work will be published as *The Qur'an: A Verse Translation*, by Liveright, an imprint of W. W. Norton, New York.

16. Shawkat M. Toorawa, "*Surat Maryam* (Q. 19): Lexicon, Lexical Echoes, English Translation," *Journal of Qur'anic Studies* 13, no. 1 (2011): 25–78.

17. Kermani, *God Is Beautiful*, 222 (see note 5 above).

CHAPTER 6   The Politics of *Koran* Translation

1. By comparison, according to *The Economist*, over 100 million Bibles are sold or given away for free every year in the world, making it the most widely distributed and best-selling book in the world.

2. See http://www.qurancomplex.org for the King Fahd Complex self-statement about their activities. Its scope and influence have also been discussed in Gary Bunt's numerous publications on Islam and the Internet (see, e.g., his chapter, "Islam and Cyberspace," in Jeffrey T. Kenney and Ebrahim Moosa, eds., *Islam in the Modern World* (London: Routledge, 2014). Bunt has also indicated the added feature of its portal. "The King Fahd Complex for the Printing of the Holy Qur'an is quite an interesting online portal, given that it is positioned alongside other translations. Its Qur'an versions online have their foundation in Harf Information Technology's development of services, and Harf also has numerous products in the market" (personal communication on November 11, 2015).

3. Although most Internet references are to the Yusuf Ali translation recycled and modified by Amana, it is crucial to note that the 1937 original version can still be located online: see http://www.sacred-texts.com /isl/yaq/index.htm (accessed on October 8, 2016). The 1937 version of Abdullah Yusuf Ali, though with God de-translated to Allah, can also be found in numerous online websites, among them Tahrike Tarsile Qur'an, Inc., at http://www.Koranusa.org/Quran .asp. Only the sacred-texts.com website sets forth the complicated copyright story of Yusuf Ali's translation, mainly so that the monitors of this website can

protect themselves against a lawsuit. "The Yusuf Ali English text [explains the webmaster] is based on the 1934/1937 book, *The Holy Qur'an, Text, Translation and Commentary* [published in Lahore, Cairo, and Riyadh]. This version is widely used because it is a clear, modern and eloquent translation by a well-respected Muslim scholar. The English text was revised in 2009–10 to more closely match the source book. But please note: The English text presented here was free of copyright in the US until 1996, at which point it had a pro-forma copyrighted status created which will last until 2033. However, in many countries, including its original country of publication, Pakistan, this text is currently in the public domain. Here's how this happened. Yusuf Ali died in 1953, and Pakistan [his country of residence] has copyright rules of life plus 50. So the Pakistan copyright expired in 2003. The Ali Qur'an English text was first published in the US in 1946, but it was never registered or renewed, and so it was never copyrighted in the US."

4. Khaleel Mohammed, "Assessing English Translations of the Qur'an," *Middle East Quarterly* 12, no. 2 (2005): 58–71. Even though the entire essay by Mohammed is weighted toward post-9/11 concern for the public awareness of, and backlash against, American Muslims, the assessment of individual translators is generally balanced. The one instance where he fails is in comparing M. Abdel Haleem, *The Qur'an: A New Translation* (Oxford: Oxford University Press, 2004) with Majid Fakhry, *An Interpretation of the Qur'an: English Translation of the Meanings* (New York: New York University Press, 2002). Both

are done by Muslim academics, but Abdel Haleem is
a more rigorous endeavor, and he is also much more
closely attuned to modern sensibilities, as Mohammed himself admits when he states: "Noteworthy
is the fact that throughout, the translator renders
the Arabic *Allah* as God, an astute choice, since the
question of why many Muslims refuse to use the
word God as a functional translation has created
the misconception for many that Muslims worship
a different deity than the Judeo-Christian creator.
Abdel-Haleem has done a good job. If any Qur'anic
English-language translation might stand to compete
with the Saudi-financed translations, this Oxford
University Press version is it" (68).

5. Khaleel Mohammed, "Assessing English Translations
of the Qur'an," 65.

6. See chapter 3, "The South Asian *Koran*," for exploration of Asad's distinctive background and approach.

7. Tauseef Ahmed Parray, review of *The Qur'ān: The
Final Book of God—A Clear English Translation of the
Glorious Qur'ān* by Dr. Daoud William S. Peachy and
Dr. Maneh Hammad Al-Johani, 2012. Qassim, Saudi
Arabia: World Assembly of Muslim Youth, *Al-Bayan*
11, no. 2 (2013): 157–59.

8. William Peachy, "Qur'an Translator Should Maintain
Clarity in Favor of Audience," speech given at 23rd
Tehran International Qur'an Exhibition, Tehran,
July 3, 2015, cited at http://www.iqna.ir/en/News
/3323007, accessed on August 12, 2015.

9. There are at least two passages in the Qur'an where
the sense of the text and also the context suggest that
al-islam should be translated as "submission" not as

Islam. Q 39:22, Peachy and Johani render the opening phrase as: "Is the one whose breast God has opened to submission?" and then in a footnote (f. 253) add: "i.e., Islam," and again in Q 61.7: "And who does greater wrong than he who invents a lie against God while having been called to submission (in Islam)?" A modernist scholar like Abdel Haleem does not even cite the "Islam" option. In both cases he renders *al-islam* with an English equivalent, either "devotion": "What about the one whose heart God has opened in devotion to Him? (Q 39:22)" or "submit": "Who could be more wrong than someone who invents lies against God when called to submit to Him?" (Q 61:7). Neither of these options would suit a traditionalist, but even more broadly what they imply is that the Qur'anic text itself allows for multiple interpretations in contemporary English idiom.

10. See chapter 7, "The Graphic *Koran*."

11. On Sells's distinctive intervention, itself a major advance in translating the early Qur'anic chapters, and the controversy from both fundamentalist Christian and politically conservative groups, see the excellent summary online at http://www.religioustolerance.org /isl_unc.htm (accessed on January 11, 2016).

12. Many of the websites that featured these translations are now defunct, but if one logs on to www.salaf .com, it's possible to trace the Qur'an translations recommended at the sidebar html at: http://www .thenobleQur'an.com/sps/nbq/ (accessed on October 8, 2016). In every instance the translation reflects prejudicial interpolations of the Arabic text, not least for Q 1:7, where Jews are taken to be the party who

caused anger, Christians those who deviated. In his oft-cited commentary, the tenth-century scholar Abu Ja'far at-Tabari has refuted both glosses, as I have demonstrated elsewhere: Lawrence, *The Qur'an: A Biography*, 86–91.

13. Toby Lester, "What Is the *Koran*?" *Atlantic* (January 1999): 43–56. The cover story for that issue, "What Is the *Koran*?" is also available online at http://www.theatlantic.com/magazine/archive/1999/01/what-is-the-koran/304024/.

14. See Garry Wills, "My *Koran* Problem," *New York Review of Books*, March 2016, at http://www.nybooks.com/articles/2016/03/24/my-*Koran*-problem/.

15. The most notable of Neuwirth's publications beyond IIS/OUP is the monumental, collaborative endeavor, Angelika Neuwirth, Nicolai Sinai, and Michael Marx, eds., *The Qur'an in Context: Historical and Literary Investigations into the Qur'anic Milieu* (Leiden: E. J. Brill, 2011). It is hard to imagine another work that so squarely and eloquently places the Arabic Qur'an within Late Antiquity, anchoring it "as a transitional text that needs to be relocated within a complex, religiously and linguistically pluralistic milieu of origin" (5).

CHAPTER 7 The Graphic *Koran*

1. There is a brief reference to Birk's endeavor "to create a personal Qur'an" in a 2012 article that also includes five panels from the title pages of what became *American Qur'an*. They are: Q 13, 22, 92, 93, and 17. The elements of Birk's artistry are evoked, though only in the last (Q 17 "The Night Journey") does the background picture

exceed the border of the page, a device highlighted to good effect in several other panels. Sandow Birk, "Artist's Statement: American Qur'an," *Journal of the American Academy of Religion* 80, no. 3 (2012): 581–86.

2. From a conversation with the artist on April 20, 2016, often referred to below. The conversation focused on the Qur'an project and the related American Mihrabs project. In what follows, all citations of Birk not marked with an endnote come from that extended, wide-ranging conversation. It did not veer into what one local reporter called Birk's "ambitious, controversy-courting art career." Nick Schou, "San-dow Birk's *Koran* Project Continues His Ambitious, Controversy-Courting Art Career," *OC Weekly*, March 16, 2016. While I agree that Birk is ambitious, I would argue that it is ethical high-mindedness, or moral in-dignation, or a combination of both, that fuels his tal-ent as also his choice of topics, along with the evident need to relate his sporting activities (skateboarding and surfing) to the everyday life of most Americans. Birk compares himself to Asad in this brief remark: "It seems that his [Asad's] works attempt to achieve a meditative connection or representation of the divine, whereas my works do the opposite—*depicting the banal aspects of daily life in juxtaposition with the divine text*" (emphasis mine).

3. For a further overview of his motives, travels, and tech-niques, see http://www.sandowbirk.com/paintings /recent-works/. *American Qur'an* was published by Liveright, an imprint of W. W. Norton, in November 2015, little more than a year after Birk finished his decade-long project. It features essays by two noted

American Muslim scholars, Cornell art historian Iftikhar Dadi, and Yale Islamicist Zareena Grewal, as well as a preface by best-selling author Reza Aslan.

4. For the 2014/15 exhibits of *American Qur'an* in Los Angeles and San Francisco galleries, Birk provided a bibliography, which he also shared with me. It included these items on Qur'an translation, some with explanatory notes.

   1. "The *Koran*" based on the original translation by J. M. Rodwell,1861. Random House, New York, 1993.
   2. "The Message of the Qur'an," translated and explained by Muhammad Asad. Dar al-Andalus Ltd., Gibraltar, 1980. (For its excellent summaries, arguments, and historical backgrounds on each sura.)
   3. "The Qur'an—A New Translation," by Thomas Cleary. Starlatch Press, USA, 2004. (For its clarity in organization.)
   4. "The Qur'an: A Biography," by Bruce Lawrence.
   5. "The Meaning of the Qur'an," Syed Abul A'la Maududi.
   6. "The Qur'an—The Noble Reading," by T. B. Irving, published by the Mother Mosque Foundation, Cedar Rapids, Iowa [and later by Amana Books].
   7. "The *Koran*—A Very Short Introduction," by Michael Cook.

There are other items in the same bibliography that background illuminated art and Arabic calligraphy, but the above are Birk's principal resources for translating the Qur'an into English.

5. I did not ask the artist about each translation decision he made in my April 20, 2016, conversation with him. What follows here, and in several endnotes, are my close readings and likely conjectures of his sources. I have also included the word/verse order of each chapter, in order to show his possible sources. In this instance, Rodwell is the likely antecedent for the *basmala*, while Wahiduddin Khan is a possible source for verse one since he also has "*The* Lord of the Universe," but since Birk often modifies Cleary in what follows, Cleary is the more probable source.

6. Although Yusuf Ali does not add the definite article to the second name, instead giving: "Most Gracious, Most Merciful." None of the extant translators has "Most Gracious, *the* Most Merciful."

7. E. H. Palmer, *The Qur'ān, Translated*, Sacred Books of the East Series, ed. F. Max Muller, vols. 6 and 9 (1880–1882), was the first to suggest: "Guide us *in* the right path."

8. This would be a rare instance where Birk uses Abdel Haleem, yet it is the source that most closely matches Birk's rendition of this critical verse. Although Abdel Haleem is not listed in the above bibliography, Birk could have seen Abdel Haleem in one of the online sites that he consulted.

9. The last verse of the Opening also invites scrutiny since Birk consciously omits the second-person pronoun: "those who have deserved Your wrath, nor of those who have gone astray." In this omission he is literally correct, since it is not there in the Arabic Qur'an. Here Abdel Haleem seems to be his model: "the path of those You have blessed, those who incur

no anger and who have not gone astray," though the rendition "wrath" instead of "anger" echoes Yusuf Ali.

10. Of the fifty-four translators listed in islamawakened .com, not one begins with the phrase "right before them is the dead earth." Instead, most prefer to render the Arabic word *ayah*, which also means verse, as "sign" (Rodwell: "the dead earth is a sign for them"). The sense of the verse, however, has been captured idiomatically by Birk, and in language that most Americans would readily grasp.

11. See Muhammad Asad, trans., *The Message of the Qur'an* (Bitton, England: Book Foundation, 2003), 758, n. 1, and also appendix 1 on "*Al-Muqattaʿat*," 1133–34.

12. Especially in Q 36:4 Birk echoes the ethical import of *sirat mustaqim* as "a right path." Yet he further shifts the accent by preferring "*the* right path" with the definite instead of indefinite article, perhaps to parallel its usage earlier in Q 1 "The Opening": "Guide us in *the* right path."

13. Djinn in Q 114:6, for example, is the sole occurrence of that word in *American Qur'an*. Elsewhere the Arabic word is translated as Sprite (Q 72 title) or spirit(s), throughout Q 72 and also in Q 6, 7, 11, 17, 18, 23, 27, 32, 34, 37, 41, 46, 51, and 55. The choice of terms for Ayat al-kursi (Q 2:255) also seems forced. While it is laudable to have a gender-inclusive rendition of this crucial, recurrent verse, Birk begins by following the lead of Cleary and uses the third person singular masculine pronoun only once in the first part: "Neither slumber nor sleep seizes Him." However, in subsequent clauses he constantly resorts to this pronoun, blunting the power of the Arabic while also forgoing consistency in

the transcribed text. On the many uses and meanings of Q 2:255 Ayat al-Kursi, see Bruce B. Lawrence, *Who Is Allah?* (Chapel Hill: University of North Carolina Press, 2015), 34–35.

14. The personal register of this panel is keen for me; it elides both my labor and Birk's with national politics. Summer 2016 marks the end of what has been for me an engrossing five-year book project. A few months later, in November 2016, one year after the publication of *American Qur'an*, a ten-year exhibit/book project, there occurred an American presidential election. Signaling both ends as also new beginnings is Q 61. Here we see the site of political conventions as battle lines, with each state and its citizens having a stake in the outcome. It is an image that dominated the summer headlines in 2016 America, merging the ethical with the visual message of Q 61 and enhancing the import of both.

15. Zareena Grewal, "How to Read Over Sandow Birk's Shoulder: An American Muslim's Notes on the American Qur'an," *American Qur'an*, xii. Throughout this chapter I allude to issues discussed, and often adapt phrases used, in Grewal's informative essay.

16. This observation, along with others in chapter 7, comes from the hour-long video of a March 28, 2016, talk that Birk gave at the University of Michigan in the distinguished speakers series sponsored by the Islamic Studies Program. For the full speech, with multiple selections from *American Qur'an*, see https://www.youtube.com/watch?v=yPbTl1EYFpE& feature=youtu.be (last accessed on October 8, 2016).

17. The instances of Birk's accent on communications are almost too numerous to cite exhaustively. Early

major panels include: Q 14 "Abraham," with electricians repairing phone lines, Q 17 "The Night Journey," with travelers at an airport, and, in a later panel for the same chapter, newspapers being prepared in a newsroom before home delivery, and especially Q 20 Ta Ha (one of the few instances where he cannot and does not translate Arabic letters into English), three successive panels: a newsroom featuring a major public announcement, with TV cameras, microphones, and satellite dishes on display, then the liftoff of a space shuttle in panel two, followed by a movie crew in a studio filming the scene from, what else?, the recreation of Adam and Eve in the mythical garden of Eden.

18. See http://www.sandowbirk.com/paintings/recent -works/ for this and several other statements from the artist/creator of *American Qur'an*.

19. Nick Schou, "Sandow Birk's *Koran* Project Continues His Ambitious, Controversy-Courting Art Career," *OC Weekly*, March 16, 2016.

20. Catharine Clark, "The Development of Sandow Birk's *American Qur'an*," in Birk, *American Qur'an*, 436.

21. There have already been ten exhibitions of *American Qur'an*. First in California (2009), then New York (2010), then back in California (2011), before Pennsylvania (2011), Iowa (2012), Colorado (2013), Washington (2014), followed by two more exhibitions in California (2014 and 2015), and finally, the tenth exhibit in Oregon (2017).

22. See Kermani, *God Is Beautiful*, 222–23. "The structure of the work (as a whole) is not important; *the quality of the Qur'an is judged from the findings on its individual verses*" (emphasis mine).

23. Among several others is Q 42 "Council," where two panels suggest a causal link, the first of a UN Assembly meeting "a council" in New York City, and then in the second panel an expanded patrol, with not just a tank and gargled soldiers but also a helicopter flying overhead, clearly over an Iraqi city, its locale signaled by Arabic lettering on storefronts. Other examples include the atomic bombs on Nagasaki and Hiroshima (panel 4 in Q 26 "The Poets"); soldiers on patrol in Iraq (Q 27 "The Ants"), another patrol sequence in Q 33 "The Confederates." Further, as previously mentioned, there are American troops that surround the border of Q 47 "Muhammed." Its two panels cover four pages. They show troops on a reconnaissance mission in Iraq after a roadside bomb has exploded, killing one of their party. A motorized vehicle has Arabic letters to translate the message: "Danger—stay back!"

CONCLUSION

1. For Wright's views on "evolution," see the preface, n. 16.
2. Cotter, "Sandow Birk: 'American Qur'an,'" (emphases mine).
3. G. Willow Wilson, "'*American Qur'an*' Is an Old/New Masterpiece." For more on Cotter and Wilson, see p. 197 n. 22.
4. There are approximately seventy instances of "*Koran*" in *American Qur'an*, not least Q 36 Ya Sin (or Human Being) discussed above. It also has cognate terms, *al-kitab* "The Book" and *al-furqan* "The Criterion," both discussed at length in the forensic analysis of Daniel A. Madigan, *The Qur'an's Self-Image: Writing and Authority in Islam's Scripture* (Princeton, NJ:

Princeton University Press, 2001). Madigan does not discuss the distinction between Qur'an and *Koran* since his own analysis is directed to the Arabic text as revealed, transmitted, and interpreted over time. Of his sources only two, Pickthall and Arberry, use the spelling "*Koran*" in their respective translations, Pickthall, *The Meaning of the Glorious Koran* (1930), Arberry, *The Koran Interpreted* (1955). For most non-Muslim Americans, however, *Koran* rather than Qur'an remains the most familiar, best-recognized name of the Noble Book, the Word of God in Arabic. See, e.g., chapter 6, n. 14, for the recent reference to Garry Wills's essay, "My *Koran* Problem," *New York Review of Books*, March 2016.

5. Like so many of the citations in chapter 7, this one comes from the personal conversation that I was privileged to have with the artist/creator of *American Qur'an* on April 20, 2016.

A page number in *italics* refers to an illustration.

English, 84, 124; spelling "*Koran*" used by, 170, 230n4; websites with translation by, 90, 91; Wikipedia's mention of, 82

plagiarism, xxii, 196n19

poetry: in Arabic, untranslatable, xvi; King James Bible and, 43; prejudice against link of Qur'an to, xvi, 106, 214n3; of Rumi, xix. *See also* aesthetic qualities; rhymed prose

polytheism, 195n16. *See also* idol worship

popular media, 132–34

prayers, five daily, 12, 15, 201n14

presidential convention, Birk's image of, 151, 156, 228n14

printing press, 33–34, 48

Progressive Islam Association, 62

progressive Muslims, collaborative translation by, 89–90

prophets: Abraham, Moses, and Jesus, 3–4, 11; false, 14–15; groups of believers in, xix–xx, xxi–xxii, 196n17; Ibn Khaldun on, xx–xxi; Muhammad as final prophet, xii, 200n8. *See also* revelation

al-Qadri, Muhammad Tahir, 91

Qadyanis, 53, 207nn5–6

Qara'i, 'Ali Quli, 88

qibla, Birk's ATM *mihrab* and, 158, 161

Qur'an: chapters beginning with isolated letters, 145;

debate about standard text of, 198n2; as Divine Will for all humankind, xii; meaning inseparable from sound of, 106–7, 117, 120; most contested verse Q 4:34, 100–103, 213n18, 214n19; number of verses and chapters in, 1; relationships between English *Koran* and, 78–80; rhetorical features of, xvi (*see also* aesthetic qualities); as sole Word of God, xi; as spoken not written text, 120; as transitional text of Late Antiquity, 223n15; verse as crucial unit for analysis of, 107, 158, 229n22. See also *Koran*; translations of Arabic Qur'an

Qur'an and Woman (Wadud), 100, 213n17

The Qur'an in Context (Neuwirth et al., eds.), 223n15

rahman/rahim, 104–5; Cleary's translations of, 110; collapsed into one by Marracci, 217n9; Toorawa on, 216n8

Ramadan, 4–5, 9, 15

revelation: to Jews, Christians, and Muslims, xix–xx; of Qur'an to Muhammad, xi–xii, 1, 4–8. *See also* prophets

rhymed prose, 105–6, 117–21; of Toorawa, 108, 117, 120, 201n14, 216n6. *See also* poetry

A Road to Mecca (Asad), 70

committee effort largely derived from, 89; copyright
story on translations of, 76,
219n3; counting *basmala* as a
verse, 216n7; impact of translation by, 64; not supportive
of Muslim state in India, 69;
original edition of translation
by, 62–64, 73, 124; Peachy on
outdated English of, 128;
photo of, *76*; Pickthall and,
63–65, 210n16; rendition of
Q 4:34 by, 99, 101–2, 213n18;
Saudi-influenced editions of
translation by, 76, *77*, 78, 90,
124–25, 131, 209n12, 209n15,
219n3; striving for exalted
tone of the original, 78, 79–
80; translation of final three
suras, 112–13; translation of
verses from Opening, 108;
translation of verses from
Surat Maryam, 118; websites
with translation by, 90, 91,
219n3; Wikipedia's mention
of, 82

Zadeh, Travis, 192n4, 194n12
Zaida, Fatma, 212n14
Zarrabi-Zadeh, Hamid, 91